LISTENING AND CARING SKILLS

LISTENING AND CARING SKILLS

A Guide for Groups and Leaders

John S. Savage

Abingdon Press
Nashville

LISTENING AND CARING SKILLS:
A GUIDE FOR GROUPS AND LEADERS

Copyright © 1996 by Abingdon Press

This book is printed on acid-free paper.

Library of Congress Cataloging-in-Publication Data

Savage, John S.
    Listening and caring skills: a guide for groups and leaders/John S. Savage.
        p. cm.
    Includes index.
    ISBN 0-687-01716-5 (alk. paper)
    1. Pastoral counseling.   2. Listening.   3. Communication—Psychological aspects.   I. Title.
    BV4012.2.S28   1996
    253'.7—dc20   96-4133

    ISBN 13: 978-0-687-01716-4

"That's Not What I Meant," the poem on pp. 25-26 is from *God Is No Fool* by Lois A. Cheney (Nashville: Abingdon Press, 1969).

Unless otherwise noted, Scripture quotations are taken from the New Revised Standard Version Bible, copyright © 1989, by the Division of Christian Education of the National Council of the Churches of Christ in the United States of America. Used by permission.

10 11 12 13 14—20 19 18 17

Contents

Using the skills in this book is limited only by your imagination. Wherever there is a need for listening, these skills can be used. They are lifewide in their application and can be used in any setting where caring is needed.

The list below of ways these skills have been used is by no means a full list, but it does represent some of the opportunities.

HOW MINISTRY TEAMS CAN USE THIS BOOK

SHUT-INS   These skills have been appreciated most by the people I have visited in hospitals and nursing homes over the years. Each of these persons has a very special story to tell, and most of the time, we hear that story only at a surface level. Through the use of these skills, you will realize that much more is being told to you than the words first imply. Shut-ins will be eternally thankful to you for paying attention to them and for listening to them with your heart.

THE TERMINALLY ILL   Hospice workers have found these skills to be some of the most helpful they have ever learned. No one is more important to hear than the dying person. Some of my most powerful times have been sitting with an AIDS patient, an elderly person, or a parent who has just lost a child. You will be able to recognize the death theme in a story, once you have mastered the skills in this book.

THE INACTIVE CHURCH MEMBER   I first used these skills in teaching people how to listen to the pain of the inactive church member. As a result of using these skills, up to 80 percent of their inactive church members have been reclaimed by some church leaders. Our attempts to listen to the church dropout had usually been futile, because we had not known how to do it. Ninety-five percent of inactive members have had a cluster of anxiety-provoking events in their personal lives before leaving the church. Listening to and responding to that cluster is extremely important in urging a person to return. These skills will teach you how to listen to pain so that it may be healed.

THE PERSON GOING THROUGH DIVORCE   Church members in my own congregation have dedicated themselves to listening to the person traumatized by divorce. Each Sunday evening, more than three hundred divorced and separated people come to be ministered to by others who have had the same experience. We have now trained more than eighty people to listen to others who are plowing through the same emotions and pain.

FAMILIES WITH A SEVERELY ILL PERSON   One church that has developed some of the most useful programs in the nation has trained more than two hundred listeners. These people work with every known affliction in the congregation. A special group works with families who have severely ill members in their midst. We often pay attention to the ill person and forget the stress and anxiety of those who are emotionally close to them.

THE UNEMPLOYED   One denomination asked an executive in their church to train more than one hundred persons to listen to the farmers in their area. They set up many listening centers throughout the state and informed all the farmers in the area that if they needed to talk to someone, a listener was available.

Another local church knew that many families in their community were affected when a large industry shut down. They visited everyone in their congregation who was laid off to listen to the pain and try to bring help where they could.

THE LISTENING CENTER   A congregation in California has set up a high quality listening center in their church. I personally trained nine people at great depth in the skills. Each of them gives four hours a week to those in their church who need a listener. A professional psychologist interviews each person before referring them to a listener, to make sure they are not pathologically ill. They are now very busy every week.

THE POTENTIAL CHURCH MEMBER   When undertaking the evangelistic task of visiting those interested in joining your church, it is important to listen to them. I believe that one should listen first and witness second. Listening builds rapport and trust. Unless you build that trust with listening, not much else is going to happen.

THE GRIEVING PERSON   A congregation in New Jersey trained thirty-four people in listening skills. The ministry they developed changed the life of their church and of the community. They visited families that had lost a member by death. They went to the home without notice, taking with them a fresh rose. They did not ask to come in, but gave the name of their congregation and said they knew that the family had lost a loved one. Attached to the rose was a card saying who they were and where they were from. After several years of visiting the grieving in all religions, their church became known as "the Caring Church" of their town.

THE TRAUMATIZED PERSON   When a tornado causes havoc in a town and people are left without homes, they not only need assistance in rebuilding, but they also need someone with whom to meet on a regular basis, so that they can tell their story. A person skilled in these listening behaviors can be very significant in helping them survive the trauma. A church in California has used these skills extensively to listen to families who have lost their homes in fires and earthquakes.

THE TEENAGER   One of the churches we trained not only listened to teenagers but trained them to train other teenagers. When this church provided three teenagers to teach these skills in one of their summer church camps, it was so successful that they did it three years in a row. Parents need to learn how to listen to their children, regardless of their age. The greatest gift you can give your children is to pay attention to them and listen intently.

MARRIED COUPLES   In a workshop we call The Couple's Connection, my wife and I have taught many couples how to listen to each other. If there is any skill needed by both persons in a marriage, it is the skill of listening. The dialogical communication which occurs when persons listen to each other while sharing their concerns or deepest love is truly enhanced by the skills in this book.

TRAINING PROFESSIONAL COUNSELORS   A man with two earned doctorates in psychology came through our skill training. He sent me a letter after the event, stating that he had taken more than sixty courses in psychology, but nothing was as useful and rewarding in his private practice as the skills he learned in Calling and Caring Ministries. I trained more than fifty counselors in Florida who were part of a denomination's counseling network throughout the state. Counselors who come to our training find these skills as useful as anything they have ever learned.

TRAINING TOP-LEVEL EXECUTIVES

Several of our advanced graduates now teach these skills in top-level industry. One such person trained more than 325 people in one multibillion dollar industry. Several years ago, I personally trained the top managers at IBM. I also spent three days with twenty principals of high schools, teaching them how to listen to teachers and students. At another time, I spent a week with the entire faculty of a college, teaching them these skills, so that they could listen to one another and the students they were teaching.

TRAINING PASTORS AND OTHER CARING PROFESSIONALS

I have trained thousands of pastors across the years, in more than forty denominations. All pastors who step into the pulpit must know how to listen to their parishioners. If you don't know how to listen, you will miss some of the important feedback, which can give you early clues about things that are about to go wrong in your church. Knowing how to effectively respond to conflict and criticism are career-saving skills. This book can help you do that. Many nurses and doctors, welfare and social workers, have incorporated these skills into their work to make them more effective as professionals.

PERSONAL USES AS A MINISTRY TEAM

I urge you to learn these skills one at a time—not all at once. For example, work on the skill of paraphrase, and practice paraphrasing with different people for a week or more. By using the skills one at a time, you can then begin to bring them together.

Many of the skills have practice sessions at the end of the chapter. Fill in those parts that ask for your response. It allows you to slow down the learning process and understand the skill.

It is extremely important to verbally practice the skills with another person, while a third person watches and then gives you feedback. When you are getting feedback, you can use the skills at that very instant. When someone is critical, it is a good time to use the skills of paraphrasing, fogging, or negative inquiry.

This book will bring you a set of skills that will enhance your own life and give you a chance to minister in a wonderfully new and healing way. Being an effective listener is one of the greatest gifts you can ever give to another.

T he framework for this book is centered on the gap that is created in interpersonal communication. The gap is produced as a result of what my brain perceives as reality in the external world and its interpretation of both the internal and external environment.

From a theoretical framework, this gap is a result of trying to interface between two worlds. One is the external world that I perceive through my senses. The second is the inner world of my brain, where I must constantly interpret both that which is going on inside me, as well as attempting to bridge the gap that occurs when I try to make contact with the outside world.

I THINK I KNOW WHAT YOU MEAN

The Interpersonal Gap

A healthy way of building a bridge over this gap is to respond to the world that is both outside and inside of me. It is quite possible to deny or to avoid both. It is also feasible that I can distort, through misinterpretation, both of these worlds that I am required to live in.

MISINTERPRETATION OF SENSORY INFORMATION

There are at least five different ways to receive information from the interpersonal communication I have with other persons. (I am limiting this discussion to interpersonal and intrapersonal inner actions, and therefore am not considering the world at large. I will include, however, relationships with groups, both small and large, and the interface between myself and these larger groups that interrelate.)

DIRECT AND OPEN FEEDBACK Communication in healthy relationships is open and direct. It does not have dissolutionary characteristics, nor is the information hidden. The persons involved in the communication process give information to each other. This disclosure is not only shared, but the accuracy is checked out by both parties, to make sure that understanding has been correctly perceived. The communicators may be using skills that are demonstrated in this book as a way to reduce misunderstanding.

11

OPEN BUT PARTIAL COMMUNICATION Communication also can take place when the speaker shares openly, with reality-based information, but leaves out part of the information. When information is left out, the listener is required to fill in the missing information with inference. *Inference* means that you presume that you know the speaker's intention, even though the speaker has not said what it is. This often takes place when the storyteller does not believe that the listener is worthy, or when the listener is unable to hear all of what the speaker has to say. Frequently, this hidden information is deep personal information that is shared only with those who have built trusting relationships.

Usually the listener believes that what is said is truthful and that the person has told all that has happened. Over a long period of time, however, this type of "secret keeping" can be dissolutionary because the listener believes (infers) that nothing has been kept back. The interpersonal gap can become significant, though it may take a long time to build.

DISTORTED FULL INFORMATION This form of interpersonal gap represents information and emotions sent to another person in which the communication is complete, but filled with distortions and misperceptions. These distortions come from incorrectly decoding the message of another but believing that what has been received is correct. The listener may misinterpret, misquote, misread, and misconstrue what the speaker is sending.

Even if the listening skills developed in this book are used, the listener may have difficulty telling what is reality-based and what is distorted information. If the listener is able to persuade the speaker to move toward behavior description, there is a better chance that there will be less distortion.

As an example, someone comes to you and says, "There are a number of people here in this office who are not happy with the way you are treating them, and I thought you should know." This kind of information has missing (deleted) information. If you ask who it is that is upset with you, the speaker may not want to say, for fear of being quoted. When this type of communication takes place, it forces the listener to infer much of the missing information, such as, who is it that is upset? What are they upset about? How long have they been upset? What did the listener do that made people upset? Any number of other self-interpretation processes also may be present.

It is difficult to be open and have clean communication if much of the information is distorted.

DISTORTED AND PARTIAL INFORMATION   This communication process is frequently experienced. The person distorts the message by giving you wrong information and, at the same time, deletes particulars, so that you are required to fill in with your own inferences. If you believe that your inferences are correct, then you add to the distortion, because neither of you is basing your information on reality.

The creation of this type of scenario leads to what we commonly call rumor. Rumor is information based not on reality but on conjecture and assumptions that have no historical base. This form of communication creates a world of nonreality. It projects onto other people the speaker's inner world, and that inner world has little or no relationship to what is going on in the speaker's environment. In this form of interpersonal communication, the gap is immense, because the intent of the speaker and its assumption by another have very little relation.

A classic example of this type of communication may help:

> Bill is sitting on the front step of a small grocery store, waiting for his wife to drive around the block to pick him up. He has just purchased some groceries and is sitting with the bag in his lap.
> Jim walks by and notices that Bill is tearing, and the tears are running down his cheeks. Jim does not say anything to Bill, but quickly walks past. Jim says to himself, "I wonder what's making Bill so sad. I bet I know—he and his wife are not getting along very well lately, and they must have been having a fight."
> As Jim walks on down the street, he sees Ralph coming toward him and says to Ralph, "I just saw Bill crying, down in front of the grocery store. I bet he and his wife were having a fight again."
> Ralph responds, "Yeah, if that keeps going on, I bet they'll be headed for a divorce."
> Ralph walks across the street and sees Betty. He walks up to her and says, "Did you know that Bill and his wife are going to divorce?"
> And so it goes.

If you had tested reality by talking to Bill to find out why he was crying, he would have told you that the onions in the grocery bag were making him tear.

NO VERBAL COMMUNICATION   The communication styles above involve greater and greater degrees of false impressions apart from a reality base. The listeners are required to create their own internal world. This world is made up of inferences, conclusions, deductions, and conjectures, all mostly fictitious in nature, and now heightened to dubious levels of understanding.

This final explanation of the interpersonal gap represents a communication mode that exaggerates the gap to its greatest distance. When no intentional communication takes place that intends to create understanding, the parties can shut off all verbal interaction.

You are at a meeting. George, who was actively participating in discussion, suddenly becomes quiet. You see that his face has become slightly rosy in color, his lips are pinched together, and the tapping of his pen on the table doubles in tempo. As a result of his withdrawal, you now are likely to go inside yourself and draw some conclusions.

You might say to yourself, "Uh-oh, I just said something that made George mad. He's so touchy, you have to weigh every word you say around him. If that's the way he acts, the heck with him. He can just be angry."

As a result of your inner dialogue, you turn away from George and no longer have eye contact with him.

If you had shared with George your awareness of what you saw, you would have a better chance of understanding what had just happened to George. There is, of course, no guarantee that George will tell you what is going on. He may, in fact, operate on the above communication styles two or three. In that case, you still would not know for sure whether you were getting reality-based information. George could simply say that there is nothing wrong and deny within himself his own awareness of why his physiology changed.

On the other hand, there is a good possibility that George would simply say that he was still struggling with something that happened at home. That his teenage son had sworn at him, and he did not have time to talk with him before he (George) had to leave for this meeting. As a result, he was still upset inside. It actually had nothing to do with the meeting or what anyone had said to him. (See chapter 7 on Behavior Description.)

A common experience I often have in working with people in listening skills is that they believe that I will know when they need me without their saying so. I recently received a letter from a rather angry participant because I did not talk with him at the workshop I was leading. He had waited around at the end of a training event to talk with me. I was busy packing up my materials and needed to leave quickly, to be driven to another training event several hours away. He did not approach me or verbally communicate with me.

In his letter, he stated that I was not sensitive to his needs because I had talked to others in the training event but I had not talked to him, and he found me an uncaring person. The fact that I was teaching this particular group how to care for others through listening made this assumption even more potent. His belief system (inference) does not match reality. No leader, no pastor, no caretaking kind of person can meet all the needs of their group.

One person can care for about ten to twelve persons in an organization. Most people do not have enough time or energy to care for more at any one time. It is possible to rotate those ten to twelve over a period of time, but most of us are limited in caring for more in a volunteer organization.

FIVE STYLES OF COMMUNICATION

1. **Direct and Open Feedback**

   Communication takes place openly and completely between parties or groups. Energy is produced and feelings are positive or resolved. Data is checked for accuracy. The relationships are productive and useful.

2. **Open but Partial Communication**

   Communication takes place openly, but some key information is left out. What is communicated is checked out, but the listener is left making some assumptions around the missing information. Or the listener assumes that what was said was complete.

3. **Distorted Full Information**

   Communication is fully developed, but many distortions of reality are present. The listeners either are forced to believe the distortions as reality or must fill in their own inferences.

4. **Distorted and Deleted Information**

   This mode of communication requires listeners to fill in large gaps of information from their own assumptions. Because much of the information is distorted, the listeners may have difficulty trying to decide what is reality-based and what is projection or conjecture.

**5. Nonverbal
Communication**

Communication of the verbal style is cut off completely. Individuals expend considerable energy in denial activity. The listeners are left with only inferences, assumptions, and conjectures, which may not have any reality base.

CLOSING THE INTERPERSONAL GAP

One of the purposes of this book is to help the reader find skills that can help to close the interpersonal gap. This part of the discussion will therefore consider other aspects of the gap and how the listening skills that follow can help to reduce possible errors in communication.

Four things are inside the sender of the communication when information is being sent to another: (1) feelings; (2) intentions; (3) attitudes; and (4) thoughts. These four attributes are private. This means that I, as the listener, cannot know what they are in any direct way. I cannot plug my nervous system into your nervous system and feel your feelings. I cannot know, in a genuine way, what your inner intentions are. Your attitudes are not knowable to me in any direct way, for I cannot be sure of what you believe about the world, and certainly I am not capable of knowing what you are thinking.

In order for the speaker to communicate about those private inner states and conditions, the speaker must produce a set of behaviors that are public. Those public behaviors take form in three primary communication modes: (1) words, which represent 7 percent of the total communication; (2) tone of voice, communicated along with the words, or independent of words, represents 38 percent of what is communicated; and (3) body language, 55 percent of the total communication process.

These three areas provide the means by which people transmit information from inside themselves to the external world. This process is called *encoding*, converting into a coding process the messages being sent by the speaker. When the receivers hear and see the other's communication, they must *decode* that message and figure out its meaning. The message sent by the speaker affects the listeners and triggers four things within the listener that are similar, but not identical to those of the speaker. Those four processes are also private in the listeners and cannot be known by the speaker in a direct way.

The listeners' private inner responses are: (1) the *feelings* that are fired off as a result of the stimulation of the environment—that is, the communication of the speaker; (2) the *inferences* that are drawn by the listeners about what they believe the speaker intended to communicate; (3) *attitudes*, which represent the beliefs and points of view of the listeners and act as filters regarding the meaning of the message of the speaker; and (4) *thoughts*, which often include the inner dialogue that goes on privately within listeners while the other is speaking.

THE PROBLEM OF DECODING

The major interpersonal gap occurs when the listener infers something different from what the speaker intends. It is quite possible to decode different messages from the same encoded message. For example: You get a call from a friend at your church, saying that two persons want to come and visit some evening during the next week. They want to spend an hour with you. Your friends do not tell you why they want to come, and you are left to infer their intention. You can decode their purpose in a variety of ways.

1. They are coming to ask you for money for the organization.
2. They want to ask you to do a job.
3. They are coming to ask you for advice about a project.
4. They are coming to scold you for not being at their meetings.
5. They want you to support them for offices they are running for.

You can go on with this list and name your own inferences.

It is also quite possible for the speaker to intend many different things in order to get the same results from the listener.

The speaker wants the listener to know that she is a competent leader. To get that intention across, the speaker may:

1. Tell you how much she received for her last speaking engagement.
2. Tell you that she has been invited by the president of a big agency to speak at their national meeting.
3. Hand you a newspaper article about her latest accomplishment.
4. Invite you to view her latest videotape.
5. Let you know that she has been invited to be a guest on a late-night television show.

It should be clear that no intention will guarantee the correct inference, and no inference will guarantee that it represents the correct intention. Because of this potential gap in interpersonal communication, it is important that the listener feed back to the speaker what she received. These feedback methods provide an orderly way of assuring that what is being sent is also that which is being received.

This book is a way to teach you some of these methods. I call them "In-depth Listening Skills." This simply means that there are many ways to give information back to the speaker in order to check out your comprehension. In fact, these skills can provide you with such extraordinary understandings of a speaker's behaviors, that often you will know more about the speakers than they will know about themselves.

The more a speaker uses methods of communication described in the five styles above, the more it is necessary to urge listeners to use feedback skills to correct possible misunderstandings. The purpose of listening skills is to provide a means of checking out your own perceptions and test them for accuracy. These skills never reach perfection. It is possible, however, to lessen the degree of error in the messages sent.

LANGUAGE AS SYMBOL AND METAPHOR

Body and verbal language are representative of inner states of emotion and knowledge, and this produces much of the difficulty. Often, what I mean by a word or phrase and what you mean by the same word or phrase is the problem.

While I was leading a lab in Calling and Caring Ministries, a young woman left the room during one of my lectures. I was talking about "turtles" (people who withdraw when under stress or in conflict) and how they manipulate others by making them feel guilty, as a way of getting what they want from the environment. Later in the lab, I had a chance to listen to the woman to find out what my comments had triggered.

In part, it was the word "manipulate," which she interpreted differently from the way I did. I meant "to manage, or produce an effect in the other person." She thought of it as meaning to control and force others to do something they do not want to do. Since she classified herself as a turtle, she thought I was putting her down, so she left angry and resentful. After talking, we were able to come to a better understanding of why she responded as she did to what I was saying.

Since I work often with churches, frequent conflict is produced by the meaning of religious words. If I do not gather the same meaning from a word that you do, then it is possible for me to walk away thinking that you have meant one thing, when in fact you did not. For this reason, it is important to frequently check out what the other is trying to communicate.

In church settings, words such as *evangelism, saved, sin,* or *heaven* connote many different meanings. Sometimes, in my workshops, I use a list of twenty-one different definitions of the word *evangelism,* which I attribute to Dr. Wendell Mennigh (Drew Theological Seminary, doctoral dissertation, 1986). For this type of word, each community must determine its own meaning.

The interpersonal gap occurs when you use the word *evangelism* and mean one thing by it, but I bring my meaning to it and infer that my meaning is yours.

On a business trip to Nashville, I was staying close to the airport in a motel. The motel did not provide an airport shuttle service, so I called the front desk and asked, "Can you tell me how I can get to the airport?"

The clerk at the desk said, "Turn left out of the motel, go to the first stop light, and turn right . . . "

I then broke in and said, "I don't need directions. I need transportation."

She responded, "Oh, I can call you a cab, Sir." She had interpreted "how can I get" to mean directions, while I had intended "what means of transportation can I use." You may have had a similar experience.

BASIC LISTENING SKILLS FOR MINISTRY

PARAPHRASE

The first of the skills to learn is that of paraphrase. Paraphrasing is the act of saying back to the speaker in your own words what you heard the person say. It summarizes the content, and the listener is concerned only about the verbal communication. This skill does not deal with emotions unless they are mentioned by the speaker.

Paraphrasing another person's spoken communication gives you a chance to check out your perception. It narrows the interpersonal gap that may occur as a result of decoding the verbal message incorrectly. (See the section on the Interpersonal Gap.)

At first, you may think that paraphrase skill is easy, and for some it is. But for most of us, it takes a great deal of concentration. It is not possible to

The act of saying back to the speaker in your own words what you heard the person say

paraphrase what others verbally communicated to you if you did not listen to what they were saying. This means that the listener must give full attention to the speaker.

KEY WORDS: CHUNKING IT DOWN

If you have never used paraphrase as a communication skill, it will be important to go slowly and break the skill down into small units. One way of doing this is to identify the key words in the person's statements or stories. It is easier to do this than to try to remember everything that is said. By "chunking down" the verbal message into key words, you will still get the essence of what the person says.

The key words are the verbs, nouns, and adjectives, which carry the meaning of the verbal communication. When you first begin, you may want to remember only two or three of these words, and then wrap the rest of the paraphrase around them.

Let me illustrate this concept. Assume that the following statement was used in a interview. I shall then identify the key words and highlight them. The paraphrase using those key words will then follow.

"I was not able to attend the meeting, because as I was backing out of my driveway, my five-year-old daughter was swinging on her swing in the front lawn. She let go with one hand to wave at me and fell off the swing and broke her arm. I ended up having to take her to the hospital. She's OK now, but it gave me a scare when it happened."

Now I highlight the key words or phrases:
"I was not able to *attend* the meeting because as I was *backing out* of my driveway, my five-year-old *daughter* was swinging on her swing in the front lawn. She let go with one hand to *wave* at me and *fell off* the swing and *broke* her arm. I ended up having to take her to the *hospital*. She's OK now, but it gave me a *scare* when it happened."

The paraphrase could be done as follows: "You are saying that you didn't attend the meeting because your daughter fell from the swing and broke her arm. You ended up taking her to the hospital." You will note that I have picked up a number of the key words, which will remind me of the fuller message.

This is not so hard to do while reading, when you have time to pick out the words that carry the major meaning. It is more difficult when you are listening and the person is speaking rapidly. It will help to practice with some written text, and then write down your paraphrase to see if you have captured the major meaning of the speaker.

PARAPHRASE STRUCTURE

The paraphrase may have two components: (1) the stem; (2) the restating of the content by the use of key words or phrases.

The stem language is introductory language and allows you to enter the paraphrase process. These stems sound like:

> You are saying that . . .
> What I hear you saying is that . . .
> You are telling me that . . .
> If I am hearing you right, you are . . .
> Let me say what I am hearing . . .

You can create many of your own. The purpose of the stem is to give you some time to get your thoughts together regarding the paraphrase statement. It also lets the speaker know that you are attempting to give feedback on what you heard the person say.

Stems are not always needed. It is not unusual, after you have learned how to paraphrase, to simply jump right into the paraphrase language without starting with a stem.

The second part of the paraphrase is to respond with some of the key words and content of the speaker's statements. It is the purpose of the paraphrase to give specific feedback to the speaker, so that both speaker and listener can check out what has been communicated. The restatement should contain some of the words that carry the important meanings.

AN ALTERNATIVE PARAPHRASE FORM

There is a use of paraphrase that is different from those above. Some use it to check out the meaning of a person's message, rather than just the content. Most of the time, we use paraphrase as the function of feeding back to the speaker the content of the message. The alternative is to respond to the implications of the message and discover its meaning.

Another way of talking about this concept is to call it a meaning check. This is a step between paraphrase of content and a perception check, which is checking out feelings. The listener must infer the meaning of the speaker. I wrote about the interpersonal gap, often made up of inferences about what the other person meant. You, the listener, infer what the speaker means, but you never checked it out. You walk away, believing that you have interpreted the storyteller correctly, but you may have been wrong.

An excellent illustration of this phenomenon comes from *God Is No Fool*, a little book by Lois A. Cheney:

> Once I saw a little boy proudly show his mother a painting he'd made at school. She looked at it, and turned it this way and that, and looked some more. "It's lovely, just lovely," she murmured. Suddenly, she exclaimed, "Oh! I see what it is! It's a house and a tree, and there's a big sun, and . . ." The little boy grabbed the paper and, bunching it all up, he hollered,

> ### THAT'S NOT WHAT IT MEANT!

> Did you ever, oh so carefully, lay out just how things were, and how they worked, and why they worked, and then sat back satisfied? Then

you heard someone repeat what you'd said, oh so carefully, and you hardly recognized it, and your brain screamed,

THAT'S NOT WHAT I MEANT!

Did you ever pry out of your heart, your mind, a tiny nugget of how you truly felt, and then told someone, probably someone special, and then stared in disbelief as he responded wrong, all wrong, and your every pore shouted,

THAT'S NOT WHAT I MEANT!

Sometimes, smug times
When I'm talking about God
When I'm praying about God
When I'm working for God,
Sometimes, smug times
When I'm very busy
in the church
about the church
around the church
I wonder
if God isn't
sighing,
or whispering,
or saying,
or hollering,

THAT'S NOT WHAT I MEANT!

In normal conversation, the same kind of gap can occur when trying to communicate specific meanings. Words often represent different meanings to different people. You cannot always assume that what it means to you, it also will mean for someone else. It is therefore appropriate, on occasion, to say back what you think the speaker means, and check to see if you are correct.

Jerry: "I see that the project I asked you to do is not finished."

Before Jerry finished speaking, **Bob** broke in: "If you don't like how I am working, maybe you should put someone else on this job!" The conversation then goes on:

Jerry: "I don't want to put someone else on the job. I'm just trying to let you know that . . ."

Bob: "There you go again. Always putting me down and criticizing my work."

Jerry: "Bob, just be quiet for a minute and listen to me. I'm glad you didn't finish the job. My boss just told me we are scrapping the whole idea, and I was hoping you hadn't spent a lot of time working on the project. If you would let me finish my thoughts before you jump in, we wouldn't get into these fights."

Bob: "Oh! You mean you were glad I hadn't completed my work because I would have done it for nothing?"

Jerry: "Right!"

When you are communicating with another person, it is very useful to keep checking out the meaning of what the other is saying. Do not assume that what you infer is what was sent. You may be decoding the message incorrectly.

SUMMARY

There are two major ways to do a paraphrase:
1. Paraphrase of content (checking out whether the words you heard are the words that were sent).
2. Paraphrase of meaning (checking out what you think the speaker meant by the comments).

During early attempts, this skill will appear easy. Each of us has known how to ask questions, ever since we were small children: "Why?" "What's that, Daddy?" "When will we get to Grandpa's, Mommy?" We have heard these questions many times. Children ask for information, data and facts, which helps them explore the world in which they live.

As long as the child is able to ask questions, and the adults (parents, teachers, friends) allow the questions to be asked, there is a good chance that the child will continue to request information about the world. This curiosity about life and the world will allow the child to explore and grow in knowledge.

On the other hand, if the child is told, "Be quiet" or "Don't ask why," the child's curiosity about the world may be reduced. If you have a good appetite about wonder, people, the dynamics of group life, national and local interests, and why individuals behave the way they do, you will find this skill very useful and rewarding.

The art of posing productive questions is a listening skill, because it is not possible to ask an appropriate question if you have not been listening to what a speaker has been saying.

PRODUCTIVE QUESTIONS

The ability to ask questions based on: free information (ideas or feelings), deleted information, distortions (words of inclusion or exclusion), and responses to other questions you have asked

"Congruent questions" are those that are relevant to the subject that is shared by the person to whom you are listening.

When a productive question is posed, you will be especially aware of the power of the right question at the right time, to illicit the type of information you need in order to be helpful to the speaker. Productive questions become the fuel for continuing the conversation. Questions provide the listener with a way to gather more useful information, so that both the speaker and the listener may reach a deeper understanding of what is being communicated. A question is no longer "productive" if the intent of the query is to entrap, rather than to help the speaker.

POSITIVE USE OF QUESTIONS

Productive questions can be used in three different ways during a conversation—listening for free information, deletion, and verbal distortion. Each is discussed and illustrated below, and then you are given a chance to exercise the techniques.

FREE INFORMATION   By using productive questions, you can prompt the speaker's story. In other words, the questions give speakers permission to tell more about themselves, or about any subject they wish to share. While sharing their story, they often give you information for which you did not ask. Sometimes this "free information" is disclosed in the conscious awareness of the storyteller, but occasionally this information emerges from the unconscious; the speaker will not be aware of what was told. Let me illustrate:

In the following dialogue, the italic type indicates comments volunteered as free information. I then respond with questions which help to develop the information needed to benefit the speaker:

LISTENER: Hi! How are you?
SPEAKER: Fine. How are you?
    L: I'm OK. What brought you in to see me today?
    S: Oh, I just needed to talk to somebody.
    L: What is it that you need to talk to somebody about?
    S: I have some things that are bothering me. *Did you know that I just got fired from my job?*
    L: No. What happened that caused them to fire you?
    S: I've been late most days for work. *I guess they didn't know that my wife was ill, and I am the only one to take care of her.*
    L: So you got fired because you were late due to your wife being ill. How long has she been ill?
    S: Oh, three years. *She has cancer.*
    L: How ill is your wife?
    S: The doctors told me yesterday that she has only about a

30

month to live. I feel kind of numb inside. *I can't seem to function very well. The biggest problem is, now that I have lost my job, I don't have any medical coverage, and the bills are going to eat me alive.*

L: Bill, a lot of things have been happening to you. What else is going on?

S: Almost everything else is OK. *My grandson died, though. Did you know that? About six months ago. He died at birth. It almost killed my daughter, too. She never has gotten over it.*

L: Bill, you have quite a cluster of very stressful happenings. Now I know why you came in to see me.

This brief illustration gives you a chance to become aware of the nature of free information and some of the appropriate ways of responding by using questions to draw out more information.

Free Information Sets Agenda

Another important purpose of free information is that it helps to set the agenda of the speaker. Careful listeners will follow that agenda because it is the means by which persons can tell you of their deeper personal pain.

One of the errors interviewers often make is to set their own agenda, not following that of the speaker. There are, of course, types of data-gathering interviews, such as job interviews, in which the listener is acquiring specific kinds of information required for making a decision about a particular employee. I am not referring to that kind of interview. The settings to which I am referring are listening to a friend, being a counselor to another, or acting as a care-giving person in a church or hospice group.

When persons offer you free information, it is like opening a door through which you are invited to come. It is a way they give you a part of their story, but they will not tell you more unless you ask for it.

I have become aware that free information is like a doorway into the unconscious. The speaker has unlocked the door or even put it ajar, is peeking out through it, motioning for you to come in. It is now your move, to indicate your interest in following through by asking more about that subject.

It might be helpful to perceive the free information which a person hands you as a very special gift. By taking it, you give the person value. If you ignore the gift, the person might experience the emotion of rejection, which emerges from not receiving care. If, however, you receive the gift and ask more about it, the speaker knows that you are willing to talk and share more.

DELETION The second use of productive questions is to help a person fill in the missing information that comes from incomplete thoughts, known as deletion. Deletion is a hole in the communication, a statement that is generalized and leaves out specific detail.

Deletion is the brain's act of omitting specific references to facts, persons, feelings, and events that may have taken place. Through productive questions, it is possible to help a person fill in the deleted information, so that the listener and the speaker can come to awareness of what has happened or is happening.

The comments below include numerous deletions. The words in italics indicate thoughts that delete detail. I will then share the implications of these words:

"I really (1) *did not like what happened* at the (2) *meeting* last night. The (3) *chairperson did not know how* to run the (4) *meeting*, and the (5) *rest* of the group was (6) *apathetic* about what was (7) *going on.*

Each of the italicized words or phrases represents hidden and protected information. By asking specific questions, the speaker should be able to fill in the missing facts or unacknowledged feelings. Listed below are some of the questions that could be asked as a result of the deletions.

I am listing here more questions than I would ask, in order to give a number of alternatives for the sake of illustration.

(1) *did not like what happened:* What is it you did not like? What specifically happened?
(2) *meeting:* What meeting did you attend?
(3) *chairperson did not know how:* Who was the chairperson, and what is it he/she did not know about running a meeting?
(4) *meeting:* What was the purpose of the meeting?
(5) *rest:* Who else was at the meeting? Were there particular persons there that you knew?
(6) *apathetic:* In what ways was the group apathetic? What, in particular, did the group do to make you believe they were apathetic?
(7) *going on:* What do you remember happened at the meeting? What were people doing?

A listener would not ask all the questions at once, but would get responses over a period of time. The purpose is to find the information in back of the deleted information. Frequently, speakers are not aware of that which is deleted. This means that a listener's ability to ask the right questions not only gives listeners additional insights and information, but also allows the speakers to become aware of that which is deleted. The speakers' new understanding often adds additional awareness to the issues being shared and gives them an opportunity to make appropriate changes, if they so choose.

The more you listen in depth, the more you will become aware that most people have relatively little insight into their own lives. Perhaps people's lives are unexamined because no one is listening to them.

wow!

One specific way to gain some insight into one's own difficulty is to be able to have someone explore with you those areas of your life that you naturally avoid. This means that we not only avoid the external world but also the internal explorations within one's self. Frequently, these psychological blind spots are sources of our difficulties. That which is behind the dark screen of our minds still drives much of our behavior and often distorts our view of reality. The difficulty is that we do not recognize this at the conscious level.

When an individual communicates, particularly through story, the verbal language gives clues to this hidden material by using deleted language. The skilled listener is able to hear the deletion and ask questions that may help prompt the suppressed experience.

The following dialogue is an illustration of questions used to explore the deletions in a person's communication:

BILL: I have been wanting to talk with you for a long time, but it took me a lot of courage to come and see you.

JOHN: What is it that you have been wanting to talk to me about? (Other questions that could be asked here: What is happening that made you require courage to come see me? How long has it been since you have wanted to come and see me?)

B: My job isn't going very well, and I need to talk to someone about it. I'm glad I have a friend like you who knows how to listen.

J: What's happening on the job, Bill? (Or, What's not going well? Or, I'm glad you believe that you can come and see me about your problem. What is bothering you?)

B: For the past several months, I have been aware that the members of the worship committee have been avoiding me. I went to talk to several of them yesterday. Three of them were talking by the choir loft, and I thought it would be a good time to ask them about the spring concert. As I walked up to them, they looked up and saw me coming, and each one walked off in a different direction. I leave messages, but they don't call me back. I'm supposed to order all the music for the fall, but I can't get the information to be able to get it together. I'm not sure what I am doing that the others do not want to cooperate with me.

J: Who are the people who have been avoiding you? (Or, When was the first time you were aware that people started to avoid you? Or, Who in particular do you need to talk with in order to get the information for your order? Or, Is the information you are to get from these people the only thing stopping you from having your order ready? Or, Are you wanting some feedback on what you are doing that makes others avoid you?)

B: Dick Spence, Harold Wolfe, and Georgia Towner are the three people I'm referring to. Dick and Harold have always been very cooperative with me, but Georgia has turned them against me.

J: What has Georgia done that leads you to believe that she is against you? (Or, When was the first time you were aware that Georgia was not cooperative?)

B: Georgia and I were working together on the fall order. She was to tell me the titles and prices for each piece of sheet music, and I was to put it on an overhead projector. Then we were going to discuss the purchase at the worship committee meeting. As you remember, I did not have them there, and you were a bit upset with me because they were not ready.

J: I do remember that meeting. Do you know why Georgia did not give you the information you needed?

What other questions would you ask to obtain the kind of information necessary to be helpful to Bill? Say them to yourself or write them here:

DISTORTION   Distortions are understood as "the universal human modeling process by which we manipulate our perceptions and remembered experiences. This process often alters experiences in a way which will better fit our own models of the world, and it is also important in the productive processes of fantasizing, planning ahead, and enjoying works of art and literature" (Byron A. Lewis and Frank Pucelik, *Magic Demystified* [Portland, Oreg.: Metamorphous Press, 1982], p. 146).

Linguistic distortions are words of inclusion or exclusion. They represent gross generalizations in the mind of the storyteller. Words—such as *every, never, always, continually, forever, every time, nobody, everyone, no one, all the time, constantly,* and *everywhere*—typify these types of words or phrases.

These words do not allow for an exception. They act as hyperbolical statements and usually do not represent reality, but they do represent a distortion of it.

The use of productive questions is relatively easy in reference to distortion words. Simply use the distortion as a single-worded question. For example:

Bill is seated in your office and is complaining about the way you ran the last meeting.

He says, "**Every time** you run that meeting, we **never** get to discuss any of the issues. You **constantly** put things to a vote too soon. You do that **all the time.**"

Response: "Every time? Bill, are you saying that when I run the meeting, we never discuss the issues?"

The purpose of checking out the distortion word is to bring the overstatement into a realm of reality. Frequently, the distortion is an attempt to get attention through emphasis of an idea: "**No one** down at church cares whether I show up or not." "**Everyone** went on vacation but us." "You are **never** home." These statements are typical of comments that contain distortion words. It is possible to respond to each of them by repeating, "No one?" "Everyone?" "Never?"

If you employ this filter for distortion, be aware that it is easy to overuse this form of question, thus losing its effectiveness. Also, the voice tone must be relatively neutral. It is easy to load it with a sarcastic or judgmental tone, thereby escalating a conflict. Productive questions can be invoked in positive ways, but this technique is also occasionally misused or mishandled.

We have had an opportunity to look at several ways to use productive questions in a positive way. Now we want to get a feel for ways that questions can be quite negative.

As useful as productive questions can be, questions also can be used in nonproductive and blocking ways. The following types of questions are usually considered inappropriate and, for the most part, to be avoided.

INAPPROPRIATELY CHANGING THE SUBJECT   One of the frequent behaviors of the poor listener is changing the subject when it is ill-timed. If, every time speakers begin to talk about a painful event in their life, you change the subject, speakers will quickly identify your avoidance. This will be particularly true if, each time the subject comes up, you change it.

The message speakers get from your behavior is that you are not interested in talking about that particular subject. Ultimately, the speakers will get the impression that you do not care, since you are not willing to hear about something that important and possibly painful to them.

There certainly are times when it is appropriate to move to another area of discussion. This section of our discussion is to make you aware of times when the change may be ill-advised.

INVADING PRIVATE SPACE   One of the most obtrusive uses of questions is asking one that invades the private space of the speaker. Such questions usually are asking for information that is very private and personal. This search for information will feel uncomfortable when the listener probably has not earned the trust level of the speaker.

If I am a church member visiting you in your home and, after five minutes of sharing, I ask you, "I understand you only give $2.00 a week to the church. How much do you make a year?" you would most likely be offended. You probably would back up emotionally, might tell me to mind my own business, or even suggest that I leave. Personal questions can be asked, but only after you have built strong rapport with the one you are visiting.

THE LOADED QUESTION   Actually, the loaded question isn't a question at all. It is a statement hidden in the form of a question. You are asked, "You think you are a good parent, and you let your daughter go out with that guy?" That is not a question asking for information. That is an accusation, disguised in the pretext of a question.

The loaded question is frequently accompanied by a sarcastic tone and forces the speaker to become defensive. It is confrontational in nature, and therefore does not give permission for the speaker to continue. At best, you will end up in some kind of argument.

When asked a loaded question, I usually respond with a question that forces clarification: "Are you asking me for information, or are you trying to tell me something?" Try to stay nonjudgmental with your questions. You will get a better response from the speaker.

PRODUCTIVE QUESTIONS REQUIRE EFFICIENT USE OF LAG TIME

In the chapter on the overview of skills, I define "lag time" as time to use the conscious mind you have left over to think of your issues while the other is speaking. It is because you have lag time that you can ask questions. It is even possible to rehearse several different types of questions, while still listening to the other person. By using your lag time, you can better hone down a more appropriate question.

A warning should be heeded: Because you do have lag time available, you can misuse the process of framing future questions. One of the misuses is to ask questions based on your own agenda. If you wish to hear the other fully, you will need to follow the agenda of the speaker. By following that road, you are less likely to get detoured and miss the essence of the other person's message.

The careful listener will work very hard at asking helpful, productive questions. You will indicate to the other that you care and are interested in what the speaker has to share. Do you get what I mean?

We discussed three types of **positive** use of questions:

- Free Information, given to you without your asking.
- Deletion, ideas which have missing information, and you must ask appropriate questions to fill in the holes.
- Distortion, specific words of exclusion or inclusion, such as *every time*, *always*, and so on. You can use the distortion word as the question: "Every time?" "Always?"

This chapter also reviewed **negative** uses of questions:

- Inappropriately changing the subject so that the listener does not have to deal with his/her own emotions.
- Invading private space by asking questions that are too intimate for the trust level.
- Asking loaded questions by using a sarcastic tone, making a statement but putting it in the form of a question.

Be intentional with the questions you ask, and you will help the speakers share the kind of information that will help them understand their own struggles and joys.

Ask, and it will be given; seek and you will find; knock and it will be opened to you.

T he skill of checking perceptions involves four stages:
- Observing the speaker's behavioral clues
- Identifying a feeling within a context
- Making a tentative statement
- Asking a question

This chapter will develop in detail these four stages. It also will give you examples of each stage, and an opportunity to practice this skill.

PERCEPTION CHECK

THE PERCEPTION CHECK IS A CARING BEHAVIOR

The purpose of this skill is to act in a caring way toward another, by identifying the other's emotions. Often in communication, the speaker sends to the listener emotionally loaded information, but does not identify that emotion. The purpose of the perception check is to

Checking out your guess at another person's emotional state.

check out your guess at what you believe the speaker is feeling. By identifying emotionally with the speaker's feelings, you convey caring and sensitivity to the person's inner emotional condition.

Each of us lives inside our skin for our entire lifetime. The emotions that we experience often stay as private, personal information. We may wonder if anyone understands what we are experiencing. Is it possible that another person could know what we feel?

Having made the identification of those feelings, there often is a bonding that takes place between the listener and the speaker, allowing the speaker to share more deeply with the listener. Speakers are often more open to sharing some of their feelings if the listeners are capable of sharing what they believe is going on inside them, the speakers.

The perception check is a very practical skill and easily learned. As you read through these instructions, take each step of the skill, practice it, then move on to the next part.

Learn these steps, and you will be able to perform this skill. First, observe the behavioral clues sent to you by the speaker. Though you can observe all parts of the communication process (that is, words, tone, and body language), the emphasis is on tone and body language. Albert Mehrabian's research indicates that 93 percent of interpersonal communication is sent by tone of voice and body language, consisting of body movements and physiological changes.

To start the skill of perception check, you must first look and listen for the clues that send emotion. The easiest and most obvious place to watch is the face. Here are the clues to look for and the emotions they may point to:

EMOTIONAL CLUES	EMOTIONS
color change (in the dark-skinned, moisture or oil-level changes)	*sad, embarrassed, anger, passion, rage, fear*
smile	*happy, pleased, content, sarcasm*
frown	*sad, upset, disgust, quizzical, unhappy, pain*
tenseness of the skin over facial bone structure	*fear, stress, apprehension*
fullness of lips	*passion, compassion, anxiety*
pinching lips together	*hesitant, doubtful, anger*
color changes of ears	*joy, passion, fear, happiness*
color changes of neck	*anger, embarrassment, love, excitement*
corners of mouth	*sad, anxious, laughter, moody*
flaring of nostrils	*anger, rage, livid*

Other behaviors to become aware of:

RHYTHM

toe (end of foot) moves slower	*calming, comfortable, relaxed*
top (end of foot) moves faster	*anxious, agitated, impatient*
fingers tapping	*anxious, impatient, unsettled*
head nodding up and down	*comfortable, agreeable, content*
body swaying (depending on the degree of sway)	*calm, very anxious, sad, impatient*
tilt of head (downward or upward)	*uptight, arrogant*
eye movements	*(see chapter on The Linquistic Bridge)*

BODY POSITION (WHEN SITTING)

slouched	*sad, distant, remorse, relaxed*
back straight	*alert, proud, attentive, alive*
arms folded across chest	*guarded, distant, physically cold*
legs crossed	*moderately distant, closed but comfortable, protected, safe*
legs and arms both crossed	*very protected, anxious, unsure, distant*
head turned toward speaker	*engaged, open, aware, close, concerned, sincere*

head turned away from speaker — *embarrassed, shy, unsure, angry, impatient, rebellious, distant, withdrawn, detached, aloof, unconcerned, numb, remote*

BREATHING

rapid — *very anxious, nauseous, impatient, frightened, hurting, aching, despair, grief*

slowing — *calming, getting more comfortable, peaceful, gentle, pleasant, serene, placid*

EYES

increasing moisture from tear ducts — *joy, pain, fear, sadness, happy, loving, angry, grieving*

pupils of eyes expanding — *angry, enraged, anxious, exploring*

pupils of eyes contracting — *fear, afflicted, alarmed, apprehensive*

red color surrounding the skin around the white of the eye — *sad, very anxious, laughter, gleeful, suppressed anger, tearful, grief, sad, sorrowful, woeful*

excessive blinking accompanied by tearing — *crying, sad, laughter, regretful, lonely, lost*

The emotions mentioned above are only a partial list. As you observe a person's behavior, and note the clues that are being sent by the body, you will become more and more accurate with your guesses at what a person is feeling.

A simple way to practice this would be to ask a friend who is open to learning with you to go inside themselves and remember an incident in which they felt some strong emotion. Then stay with that emotion and let you guess at what the feeling(s) might be. You could also see the large variety of body clues that are given concurrently.

Rarely will you find just one clue exhibiting itself at one time. The body sends many signals simultaneously. The more you can note, the more information you will have to make a more accurate guess.

Please be aware that many of these behaviors are very subtle, and it takes considerable acuity of observation to see them all at once.

TONE OF VOICE   After seven years of professional voice training as a musician, I became aware of the great subtleties in tone of voice and quality. This next section will deal with some of the generalizations you can use in guessing at emotions by listening to voice tone.

If you listen carefully, you will note that the voice falls in a range register that can be labeled high, medium, or low. This simply means that the voice can often be heard in the upper part of the mask of the face as high, light, thin, squeaky, transparent, and so on.

High Voice Range

When the voice is high in the mask, the emotions that accompany it can be distant (including distant from one's own emotions), unconcerned, feeling good, elated, delighted, overjoyed, euphoric, excited, buoyant, ebullient, festive, exhilarated.

When the voice is in the upper part of the mask (upper cavities of the face) the person is often far removed from any specific pain. There will be exceptions—that is, shrieking when seeing something frightening, such as a snake. Most of the time, however, the individual is unaware of any deep emotions. It is as if the unconscious drives the voice upward as a means of avoiding its painful states.

Medium Voice Range

The voice is often located in the middle of the mask, when we say it sounds natural. The quality of the sound may range from nasal (when the voice is focused behind the nose) to breathy (when the voice is focused toward the mouth cavity).

Emotions that evoke these tonal qualities may range from comfortable, at ease, genial, warm, desirable, and lively, to sarcastic, mocking, scornful, belligerent, angry, vociferous, and loud. The matching or mismatching of tone and words should be observed. Often incongruence is noted in the subtle mismatching.

add the context "superintendent asking you . . . " and then add a question "any chance I'm right?" Putting the parts together, it sounds like this. "Mary, *I get the impression* that as a result of the *superintendent asking you* to take the new job, you might be feeling *a little scared* at the new responsibilities. *Any chance I'm right?*"

Let's do another one. You have just completed a meeting with one of your favorite volunteers. He's actually become a friend because you have worked side by side through lots of ministries, and you have played golf together. You know something of his family, and you personally like him. But in this particular meeting, Jim (the volunteer) is giving you a hard time about the project. Because you have become a more observant listener, you note the following:

The veins on Jim's neck bulge mildly. The skin on his upper lip becomes just slightly shiny with tiny beads of sweat, and his eyes glisten with additional moisture. The pen he is holding taps more rapidly on the table. He looks toward the floor and has moved until he is standing with his side toward you. His voice seems to be deep in his throat, and his speech is hesitant.

While you are observing this, he says, "You've got to be kidding! You think I'm going to do that for this church? I thought we were friends. I think you're trying to do me in." What do you think he is feeling? Name the emotions your guess might include.

STAYING IN THE BALLPARK OF EMOTIONS

It is important to stay within a reasonable range of emotions that you believe a person is feeling. Sometimes you may completely misread a person and name an emotion that is very incorrect. Even when you do, there is no harm done in the relationship, because the speaker will usually tell you that you are wrong, and then often mention the actual feelings.

A man is clenching his fists, getting red in the face, yelling, and slamming an object down on the table. If you then use the emotional word "happy" to describe his feelings, you will be outside the ballpark of his emotions. In fact, such a mismatch will often be perceived as sarcasm.

TESTING YOUR OWN EMOTIONS   One way of honing down the emotion, and being more accurate, is to test the emotions you are experiencing. Often our own counterstory sparks our own emotions. If you keep in touch with what is going on inside yourself while you are listening,

46

there is a better chance of guessing what is going on in the other. So be aware of your own inner condition as you are listening to the other.

A rather unusual expression of this phenomena occurred during a break at one workshop. A participant came up to me and said that he was not catching on to the idea that he could make a guess at others' feelings by getting in touch with his own.

I asked him what he had felt, and he said, "Nothing." I queried him about the story and other characteristics of the speaker. He told me that the speaker's voice was flat in tone, that there was no color or skin change, that the speaker often stared into space while he talked. Again I asked the listener what he felt.

Again he said, "Nothing."

I said, "No kidding."

He said, "No kidding."

"You didn't feel a thing, right?"

"Right."

"Guess what the speaker was feeling?"

"Nothing!"

"Right, the speaker was feeling nothing. The speaker is sealed off on the inside. He is out of touch with his emotions. Guess what you just learned about him?"

The speaker appeared to be unaware of his own feelings and had sealed them off. The listener had picked up a kind of vacuum, an emptiness. Trust your intuition.

SOFTENING THE EMOTIONAL WORDS   When you are in a low trust relationship, it is useful to reduce the intensity of the emotional word. For example, if the speaker is expressing behavioral clues that lead you to believe that the person is experiencing high levels of frustration, then it would be appropriate to reduce the intensity of the word *frustration*. Other feeling words you might use are *thwarted, stressed,* or *concerned.*

The purpose of using a less intensive word is to reduce the threat of becoming confrontive and invasive. If you lower the intensity, you will be less likely to get a denial response from the speaker. Since the objective of using the perception check is to show that you are concerned about the speaker's emotional experiences, it communicates to the speaker that you have empathy and are willing to share the deeper experiences that the storyteller is having.

Here are a few feeling words that a person may be experiencing. Listed next to them are feelings of different intensity:

Angry: frustrated, hurt, annoyed, a bit angry, upset.
Happy: comfortable, glad, joyful, content, merry
Sad: blue, bleak, sorry, unhappy
Rejected: defected, disavowed, discarded
Irritated: sore, annoyed, unhappy, unsettled

This list should give you some idea of what I am after when I talk about lowering the level of the emotion. The intention of lowering the intensity is to be sensitive to the emotional experience the speaker is experiencing.

SUMMARY

A perception check is making a guess at the inner emotional state of another person. The check is accomplished by first observing the body language, tone of voice, and verbal communication being sent to you. From those behavioral clues, you make a guess at what you believe the speaker is feeling. After naming the feeling in your head, you may want to soften it, according to the trust level you have with the speaker. You then place the feeling word into the context of the perception check, which has the following components:

STEM + FEELING WORD(S) + CONTEXT + QUESTION

I urge you to try this skill, for it can build excellent relationships.

EXPRESSION OF FEELINGS AND EMOTIONS

*Naming your own
inner emotions*

One of the most recurring problems in life is dealing with emotions. This chapter is devoted to helping you understand the nature of emotions and how better to manage them.

If I stood you on a table, tied your hands and feet, and started to push you over backward, your body would very quickly send you information about the external world. The signals are to warn you of impending danger; thus you might feel anxious or frightened.

If I held your face gently between my hands, you might feel a sense of warmth, because when you were a child, a parent or other important person told you that you were loved and wanted. That same behavior may cause you to feel sad.

While teaching these listening skills in seminary during summer school, I demonstrated that touching can bring on feelings. I asked a student, who was seated in the front row, if she would permit me to touch her face. She agreed. I placed both my hands on her cheeks, and she instantly broke into tears. I quickly stepped back and asked her what she saw as a result of my touch. She said, "Whenever I was bad as a little girl, my father used to slap me across the face."

Our feelings can be induced by many things from the external world. You recall the tone of voice of someone, and the tone reminds you of the time you were scolded by a parent or teacher, and you feel the same way you did when you were first scolded. Someone speaks to you softly, and you feel comforted or strengthened, because the tone brings back memories of being cared for by some special person.

It is not unusual to find that we are drawn toward people who elicit comfortable feelings, while we avoid those who bring out feelings of anxiety or anger.

One night my wife came home from a meeting upset and annoyed because of things some people did and said. She talked for a half hour about what happened, and I listened to try to help her find what it was that upset her. It seemed that there was considerable history of discomfort with some of the people on the committee, and that had fired off her old unresolved feelings. That is the way it is for most of us. It is not what the person is currently doing that makes us so uneasy, but what the behaviors remind us about unresolved past events.

THE SKILL OF DIRECT EXPRESSION OF FEELINGS

Definition: The skill of direct expression of emotion is naming, in first person singular, an emotion or feeling that you have experienced or are now experiencing.

Example: I feel very irritated by the committee's actions.

Purpose: The purpose of direct expression is to identify your emotional state, and name that emotion to the person with whom you are communicating.

DIRECT EXPRESSION OF EMOTIONS

For some, this skill will be very simple; for others, it will be difficult. If you are aware of your own inner emotional state, this skill will come with no effort. If, however, you have difficulty identifying the range of emotions that are in you, then this skill will be much more complicated.

In the chapter on Perception Check, I talked about making a guess at other persons' emotions. That guess was necessary because the speakers did not name their own inner condition. Instead, they sent emotions through indirect expressions. The function of direct expression is to be able to express the emotion that is going on in you. That way, the listener does not need to infer the condition. If I want you to be aware of my inner state, then I must name it, because I am the only one who knows what is going on inside me.

THE DIFFICULTY WITH EMOTIONS   Many of us have difficulty with emotions. In the most mundane sense, emotions are chemical reactions that send messages to the brain for control and safety. Anxiety is the early warning system in our bodies to alert us of possible harm or danger. Anger is experienced to motivate us to settle some difficult issue with ourselves or with some other person. The emotion of joy is useful as a means to celebrate life's experiences. Not being able to feel is to deny being human.

We are feeling creatures. God made us that way. Yet many people have sealed off their emotions so that they cannot experience them at the conscious level.

THE CONTROL ISSUE   Our emotions often seem to have a life of their own. We cannot turn them off and on at will. However, it is possible to experience them in ways over which we have more control. The more you are aware of the emotion, the more you can determine how you will act or behave. When the feeling remains only at the unconscious level, then the feelings can control behaviors that are out of your awareness. This phenomenon is called acting out. Acting out occurs when you feel driven to do something, but you do not know why. There is less acting out if you stay in touch with the emotion. If you will identify it and experience it, then there is a chance that you will have a less destructive behavior. Thus, the first part of this skill of direct expression is to notice your own inner condition. On the following page you will find a list of more than 200 "feeling" words. We use them in trying to identify the feelings of others. Many people say that they have experienced 90 percent of these feelings at some time in their life. How about you?

ACTING OUT/ACTING IN   We express our emotions in four ways. The first two ways are *acting out* and *acting in*. The other two ways are *direct* and *indirect expression through verbalization*.

Acting out is having your emotions drive your behavior. When you are not aware of your emotions, there is a greater chance that you will act on those unfelt emotions. Sometimes this is not severe enough to get you into trouble, but at other times, you do things that produce problems, and you catch yourself saying, "Why did I do a dumb thing like that?"

A classic case of acting out occurred a number of years ago with one of my former acquaintances:

A twenty-three-year-old white, unmarried woman called asking to see me because she was pregnant and considering an abortion. I set a date with her, and we discussed the problem. In that interview, I discovered that she had broken up with a boy she had dated for seven years. She claimed she

FEELING WORDS

HAPPY	SAD	ANGRY	DOUBTFUL	MISCELLA-NEOUS
bouyant	ashamed	annoyed	defeated	
brisk	blah	awkward	dubious	bored
calm	choked up	belligerent	evasive	cruel
carefree	compassion-	bewildered	distrustful	distant
cheerful	ate	bitter	helpless	envious
comfortable	concerned	boiling	hesitant	humble
complacent	disappointed	confused	hopeless	jealous
contented	discontented	cross	indecisive	mixed-up
ecstatic	discouraged	enraged	perplexed	preoccupied
elated	dismal	frustrated	pessimistic	torn
enthusiastic	dreadful	fuming	powerless	
excited	dreary	furious	questioning	**AFRAID**
exhilarated	dull	grumpy	skeptical	
festive	embarrassed	indignant	suspicious	alarmed
generous	flat	inflamed	unbelieving	anxious
glad	gloomy	infuriated	uncertain	appalled
grateful	heavy-hearted	irate	wavering	apprehensive
hilarious	ill at ease	irritated		awed
inspired	in the dumps	offended	**PHYSICAL**	cautious
jolly	low	provoked		cowardly
joyous	melancholy	resentful	alive	dependent
jubilant	moody	stubborn	breathless	dismayed
lighthearted	mournful	sulky	empty	doubtful
merry	out of sorts	sullen	feisty	fearful
optimistic	quiet	wrathful	hollow	fidgety
peaceful	somber		immobilized	frightened
playful	sorrowful	**FEARLESS**	nauseated	gutless
pleased	sulky		paralyzed	hesitant
relaxed	sullen	bold	repulsed	horrified
restful	sympathetic	brave	sluggish	hysterical
satisfied	shameful	confident	stretched	impatient
serene	unhappy	courageous	strong	insecure
surprised	useless	daring	sweaty	nervous
sparkling	worthless	determined	taut	panicky
spirited		encouraged	tense	petrified
thrilled	**HURT**	hardy	tired	pressured
vivacious		heroic	uptight	shaky
	aching	impulsive	weak	shocked
EAGER	afflicted	independent	weary	scared
	cold	loyal		suspicious
anxious	crushed	proud	**AFFECTION-ATE**	terrified
ardent	despair	reassured		threatened
avid	distressed	secure		timid
desire	heartbroken		aggressive	tragic
earnest	injured	**INTERESTED**	appealing	wishy-washy
enthusiastic	isolated		close	worried
excited	lonely	absorbed	loving	
intent	offended	concerned	passionate	
keen	pained	curious	seductive	
proud	pathetic	engrossed	sexy	
zealous	suffering	excited	tender	
	tortured	fascinated	warm	
	worried	intrigued		

was not angry with him, but had initiated the break because he could not make up his mind to marry her. It was obvious that volunteering the information was a way for her to defend against some strong anger against him.

She was also interviewed by an obstetrician. Our collaboration came to the conclusion that an immense amount of anger was being expressed in noncreative ways, since two weeks after breaking up with the boyfriend, she started to date another young man. On the second date, they had sexual relations and she became pregnant.

At my urging, the young woman returned for eight additional sessions, to see if she could work through some of those feelings that at first were not evident to her. On about the fifth session, she got in touch with that anger. It expressed itself in crying, swearing, and verbal phrases that expressed deep loss and frustration, along with a fear that no one else might like her. By the end of the eighth session, she was able to come to grips with most of her anger and seemed to be able to stay in touch with it.

(John S. Savage, *Apathetic and Bored Church Member* [Reynoldsburg, Ohio: L.E.A.D. Consultants, 1976], p. 26)

Acting out can include eating when anxious, or yelling at a child louder than necessary because you had a bad day at the office. It can be as subtle as forgetting your mate's birthday, or as blatant as getting drunk rather than experiencing and exploring the feeling of helplessness and anger. It can also extend itself to destructive behavior, such as setting up an important staff meeting and then forgetting to attend.

There is a pathological level of acting out as well. This means that the individual is completely out of touch with any feelings and can experience no remorse or guilt. This person is the pathological killer who can walk up to other persons, drive a knife into them, walk away, and not feel a thing.

Most of us fall within the first two categories. We act out on occasion, but with no great damage to our relationships. The more persons can be in touch with their emotions, the less likely they are to act out.

Acting in is another way we deal with our emotions. Acting in is quite different from acting out. Again, this is a situation in which persons are not in touch with their emotions. However, instead of having the emotions drive external behavior, the mind directs the emotions back in on the body, and the person becomes ill.

Psychosomatic illness is often a result of acting in. These physical manifestations show up in migraine headaches, peptic ulcers, lower back pain, and such ailments. You go to a doctor for help, the doctor examines you, and finds nothing wrong. Yet you complain about the pain.

The pain is just as hurtful as if there were a real physical problem, but the doctor cannot find any physical cause.

Another dimension is that "stuffing" one's emotions can cause physical and emotional illness.

In one instance, I met with a pastor and two bereaved women, both of whom had recently lost their husbands. One of the women said that she had cried every day since the funeral. She believed that her continual crying meant that she was unstable, that she should not be crying so much. The second woman responded that she had not cried at all. In following what happened to those two women, I learned that the first did her hard work of grieving and had worked through the loss. Since that time, she has married a very caring man and is doing well. The second woman ended up in a mental hospital three months later, depressed and feeling out of control. She has had difficulty getting close to another man. Getting in touch with your emotions, experiencing them, will bring you a greater sense of control and health.

INDIRECT EXPRESSION OF EMOTIONS

A third, very common means of dealing with emotions is to express the emotion but not name it. This form of expression combines verbalization, tone of voice, and body language in such a way that the emotion is communicated but not identified.

Suppose that a friend says to you, in a sarcastic tone, with the chin slightly raised, "You're a great chairperson, I can tell by the way you ran the meeting yesterday." Note that no emotion is named. The words are quite all right, but the accompanying tone and body language communicate something quite different. The incongruities and the lack of direct identification with a feeling word makes this an indirect statement. Indirect expressions can come in many forms:

- A compliment—"You are a very nice person."
- A criticism—"You never do what I ask you."
- A loaded question—"Do you think you should be doing this?"
- An Accusation—"You don't love me anymore."
- Name calling—"You bozo!"
- Judgments:
    Approval—"You're a delightful person."
    Disapproval—"All you do is talk, talk, talk."

54

The difficulty we often have with this form of communication is that we need to guess at the emotion(s) behind the statement. Often we just infer what that emotion is, and then we believe that our guess is correct. If you are the listener, then the skill of perception check is appropriate here (see chapter 3). You will recall that the perception check checks out your hunch about what the other person is experiencing. On the other hand, if the speaker states directly what he or she is experiencing, the perception check is unnecessary. If you hear me say, "I am annoyed by what you said in the meeting yesterday," you do not need to guess at what I am intending or communicating.

DIRECT EXPRESSION OF FEELINGS

A brief formula can be used in creating a direct expression of feeling: It uses first person singular, and it names an emotion or emotions.

Statements that do not conform to this formula are other than direct expressions. For example, if someone says to you, "We like what you did for us while we were on vacation," you might think that is a direct expression because of the feeling word *like* in the sentence. However, the plural "we" is not consistent with the formula, and therefore disqualifies it as a direct expression. The plural distances the speakers from identifying their own emotions, projecting them onto a generic "we." If the speaker had said, "*I* like what you did . . . ," then it would become a direct expression. The following are statements which represent direct expressions:

"I am very **upset** at what happened today."

"I struggle very much with what you said, and I'm **anxious** when talking to you about it."

"It **annoys** me that I was not informed about the meeting and missed it."

"When I received your letter, I was **happy** to hear that you got the job you had wanted."

"The constant slamming of the door **irritates** me."

"I am open to your criticism, but I am **unsure** how to respond to your remarks."

In using the direct expression, you clearly inform others about your own inner condition, so they may know why you are responding the way you are.

The following is a typical conversation, in which the listener is using direct expression with the speaker.

Linda is the listener. She is sitting in her office when Ralph, a member of her staff, walks into her office:

RALPH: Do you have a moment to talk with me?

LINDA: Oh hi, Ralph. . . . Sure, sit down.

R: It became obvious to me today that you are trying to sabotage what I am doing here. I need to find out what is going on."

L: Ralph, I'd like to hear what I did that gives you the impression that I am sabotaging you. I'm feeling **unsure** about what you might be wanting to say.

R: You were supposed to finish the project that I gave you three weeks ago. The department was depending on getting the product to our client, but you delayed it so long that now the client has canceled the order.

L: I'm really **disturbed** to hear that. Joe, from production, stopped in to see me four weeks ago and told me that the order had been canceled, and I was not to spend time doing it. I'm really **confused** when you tell me it was canceled because I did not get it done.

R: You're saying that Joe knew it was canceled a long time ago? I didn't know that. Why didn't he tell me?

L: I don't know, Ralph. You'll have to ask him yourself.

R: I'm sorry for accusing you. I had the wrong information.

Linda included a lot of self-disclosure (direct expression), while Ralph did not. Linda did two important things in this dialogue. One, she clarified a misunderstanding of information, a great cause of conflict among co-workers. And two, she expressed what was going on in her, so that Ralph did not need to guess.

Such an act of self-disclosure need not be used all the time, but it is necessary when communication requires very clear understanding, so that conflict does not increase.

Chapter 5

FOGGING

In teaching how to listen, I instruct people how to respond to criticism, one of the most difficult parts of listening. I urge them not to deny any form of criticism. If you respond with critical comments, that is just doing what they are doing. I also urge them not to get defensive or counterattack.

Manuel J. Smith, the creator of fogging, is trying to help those who are highly manipulated by others. He is attempting to give them an alternative way of responding, rather than by being defensive. He is not offering a method to foil all forms of criticism, but trying to help the listener learn appropriately from criticism.

Smith gave the name *fogging* to this skill because he wanted the person being criticized to act like a fog bank:

Naming the truth in another person's critical statements

A fog bank is remarkable in some aspects. It is very persistent. We cannot clearly see through it. It offers no resistance to our penetration. It does not fight back. It has no hard striking surfaces from which a rock we throw at it can ricochet back to us, enabling us to pick it up and throw it at the fog once more. We can throw an object right through it, and it is unaffected. Inevitably, we give up trying to alter the persistent, independent, nonmanipulable fog and leave it alone. Similarly, when criticized, you can assertively cope by offering no resistance or hard psychological striking surfaces to critical statements thrown at you.
(*When I Say No, I Feel Guilty* [New York: Bantam Books, 1975], p. 104)

I find fogging to be one of the most useful yet simple skills to learn. Of the eleven listening skills presented in this book, fogging is the easiest and most fun to master. There are several ways fogging can be done:

1. You can agree with any statement that is true for you.
2. You can agree with any statement that may contain some truth.

3. You can agree with any statement that is a generalization, as long as it has some possibility of being true for you.

FOGGING STEMS

As you are aware from other skills in this book, many of them start with what I have called a "stem." Fogging also employs this method. Following is a list of stems that are used, depending upon which kind of fog (as listed above) you are using.

- That's right.
- You're probably right.
- That's probably true.
- You're right.
- You could be right.
- I guess you're right.

When criticism comes your way, there is often a predictable response called defense. If I am the critic, and I can get you on the defensive, then I can run you all over the tennis court. As long as I am hitting you with criticism, and you are always reaching for a defense shot, then I can keep you running as long as you want to run. I am, indeed, in charge of the relationship, and you are at the end of my behavioral whip.

But I can't keep you running if you won't run. Fogging, therefore, is a behavior which says that you won't play that kind of game, so you simply respond with what you think may be true in my criticism of you, and let it go at that. Here are several brief dialogues which incorporate the fogging responses:

CRITIC: You are always late for meetings.

FOG: You could be right, I am not always here on time. (It is often helpful to add a comment after the fog, to put the fog into a context.)

C: You think you are a pretty good chairperson of our committee, but Jean did a better job than you're doing.

F: You're probably right. Jean did do an excellent job. (Agreeing with only the part of the statement that is true.)

C: I'm surprised that you want to stay chairperson, if you are doing such a lousy job.

F: I'm sure you are surprised at my staying chairperson. (Agreeing with what is obvious in the critic's statement. Notice what was omitted.)

C: Let me add one other thing. You have loaded this committee with your friends, so they will vote on everything you want.

F: It is true that the group has voted on many things I have suggested.

The fogging statement agrees only with what is true for you. If you search within a critical statement, it usually does not take long to acknowledge what part of that statement may be true. Suppose you are a manager of others at your job. Fogging can be used with great effectiveness in interactions between managers and employees.

Here is a manager who is in conflict with one of his employees. The dialogue goes like this:

EMPLOYEE: We didn't meet our production quota because you keep delaying giving us the sales reports so we know what to produce. We are all mad at you. When are you going to get your act together?

MANAGER: You might be right that production quotas weren't met this past month.

E: Yeah! And it's all your fault!

M: You may be right. I could have been more prompt getting you the information.

E: Let me add something else. You have not sat down with any of us for over a month, and I think that is what is getting you into trouble.

M: That could be our problem. I could be meeting more often with the leaders than I do.

Note that I am isolating this skill so that you can learn its language. Fogging is rarely used in isolation. It is more likely to be coupled with Productive Questions, Paraphrase, or a Perception Check. (See chapters on these skills.) The next brief example puts fogging into context with the other skills:

HUSBAND: What is this stuff that we have to go see your mother every Sunday afternoon? It's a pain. Not only that, but your mother treats you like you don't have a brain in your head.

WIFE: You're right. I have been seeing my mother a lot lately, and there are times when she does put me down. (FOGGING) I'm a little frustrated with all of it myself (DIRECT EXPRESSION OF FEELINGS), and I get the impression that you're really annoyed by it—right? (PERCEPTION CHECK)

H: So what are you, a pantywaist? Start making your own decisions, rather than always doing what your mother tells you.

W: You're saying that I should start making my own decisions and not do what my mother wants all the time. (PARAPHRASE) And you're probably right; I could be stronger than I am and not be so influenced by my mother's decisions. (FOGGING) I do feel in a bind at times between doing what Mother asks and what you want. (DIRECT EXPRESSION OF FEELINGS)

In the last comment, the fogging statement is tucked into a longer response and is hardly recognizable, in and of itself. The more inconspicuous you can make the fogging statement, the more effective it is.

Because these skills often are used by persons in caring professions—that is, counselors, pastors, welfare workers, nurses, doctors, and such, here is an example of the effective use of fogging when a pastor makes a call on an angry church member:

PASTOR: Hi, Lois, how are you?

MEMBER: Not very good. And much of it has to do with you. You certainly don't know how to take care of your congregation.

P: That may be true. I am not always able to meet everyone's needs. (FOGGING) What is it in particular that I did that seems to be upsetting you? (NEGATIVE INQUIRY)

M: I am very disappointed in you. When you first became my pastor, I felt that surely you would be able to lead this church to great things. But actually, you're a disaster area!

P: It is true that the church has not progressed as some had hoped. (FOGGING) But I wonder if there is something happening that is angering you besides what is going on at the church. Maybe with me personally. (NEGATIVE INQUIRY AND STORY CHECK)

M: Well, now that you have mentioned it . . . there is. I was very ill with a bad breast infection and was near death. I called the church office, and they said you would come to see me. They even told me later that they had given you a written note to that effect. Yet you did not come. I understand that you went off to a youth retreat, choosing the kids instead of me. The kids were healthy and could have gotten by without you, but I needed you very badly, and you did not come.

P: It is true that I did get the note about your illness and that I went with the youth. (FOGGING) I'm now aware that that may have hurt and angered you a great deal. Right? (PER-CEPTION CHECK)

M: More than you will ever know.

P: I'm feeling quite anxious as you tell me this, and I'm not quite sure what to do, now that it has happened. (DIRECT EXPRESSION OF FEELINGS) I am very sorry if I have hurt you, and I apologize and ask for your forgiveness. What would I need to do, to help you work through this broken expectation? (RENEGOTIATION)

This dialogue is not intended to produce a quick fix. It is to demonstrate how fogging can keep the pastor from being put on the defensive and manipulated via guilt. Please note that fogging is best used in conjunction with the other skills.

PRACTICE THIS SKILL YOURSELF

Write or verbalize a fogging statement after each critical statement listed below:

1. You didn't get your report in on time, and so it will not be printed in the annual report.

2. Your clothes look like you slept in them.

3. You are not taking care of yourself. Your stomach is hanging out over your belt.

4. I don't mean to be critical, but if you are late for work once more, I will report it to the boss.

5. The doctor told me that you will no longer be my nurse. You are totally incompetent.

Remember that fogging is naming the truth in another person's criticism. You identify only that which is true for you. So take this fogging skill and put it into your ongoing life. You will feel stronger and better able to deal with manipulative people.

T he skill of Negative Inquiry is one of the most useful skills I teach. I was first introduced to it in a book by Manuel Smith, *When I Say No, I Feel Guilty.* You may want to read his chapter on the subject.

The purpose of this skill is to allow you, the listener, to turn your critic into your teacher, rather than your enemy.

Most of us have some difficulty in dealing with critical people. Negative Inquiry will give you another option, so that you will be less manipulated by a critical person's behavior.

In the preceding chapter (Fogging), I talked about defusing the critic by agreeing with the truth in the critic's comments. Often, Negative Inquiry follows the Fogging statement. Let me first describe the Negative Inquiry skill, and then add it to other skills.

Negative Inquiry usually is made up

NEGATIVE INQUIRY

Coaching your critic to criticize you in specifics, rather than in generalities.

and accompanied by several other skills already described in this book. The central skill used is that of Productive Questions. Other skills that can accompany it are Perception Check, Paraphrase, Fogging, and Direct Expression of Feelings. If you have not read these chapters you may want to go to those sections before reading this. However, you may want to read about Negative Inquiry, and then go to the other chapters, to help you understand what you read here.

This skill is not difficult to learn, but sometimes is difficult to do, due to the emotional reactions you may have when being criticized. So let's explore the skill.

NEGATIVE INQUIRY AND PRODUCTIVE QUESTIONS

Negative Inquiry is the skill of asking the critic to point out your specific behaviors that are upsetting the speaker. Questions are asked, because the critic may use generalizations. This leaves the listener not knowing what to do differently, because no specific behavior has been identified. The function of Negative Inquiry is to coach the speaker to name a specific behavior, so that you know what to change, if you choose to do so.

If you are a chairperson of a committee, and one of the members tells you that you are a lousy leader, that type of feedback is not very helpful. It is what I call the Lucy Syndrome. Sitting behind her booth, Lucy gives Charlie Brown, the cartoon character, a lecture. When she is finished, Charlie Brown turns to her and says, "Now that I know that, what do I do?"

When someone gives you feedback, but does not name any specific behaviors, you have to guess at what you are doing that is causing the person to be annoyed. Negative Inquiry coaches (asks) the critic to identify specific behaviors, so that you may know what you might do differently in order to get a different response. You are actually coaching the person in Behavior Description. (See chapter 7.)

REFRAMING CRITICISM   Reframing an event is changing the meaning of an event from negative (a nonuseful attitude) to positive (a very useful attitude). When you change the frame on a picture, the picture looks different. You will find that by turning your critic into your teacher, you have an opportunity to learn how people perceive you and your behavior. By coaching your critic to name specific behaviors or patterns of behavior, you are given options to change some of your behaviors that may cause you difficulty.

This process of receiving criticism is a form of feedback which, when guided with specific skills, can turn the criticism into useful information that you, the listener, can use.

Negative Inquiry, when used properly, can save your relationship with a person you value, whether it be a friend, business associate, or client. Knowing the skill and its usefulness made me aware of the behavior of a man I had sought out while I was in the client role. I called him to express my dissatisfaction with the interest rate I was receiving on some of the investments I had made with him during the previous nine years.

When I called the broker, his behavior was very defensive, and he put down the investment company I was thinking of changing to. Then he chided me for even considering such an act. He became angry and paid scant attention to my complaint. Each time I wanted to express my concern, he would counter with more defensiveness. He told me how good a broker he had been, that I couldn't do better with the other company.

The issue became obvious to me as we talked. He could not hear my concern, nor did he try to discover the issues. When a client brings concerns to you, you had better drop your defensive behavior and listen, if you want to pursue the chance of keeping the client.

LEARNING THE SKILL   If you have read the chapter on Productive Questions, you may recall that one of the productive ways of using questions is to note the missing information that is absent in a person's story or ideas. Negative Inquiry asks questions that illicit the missing details. The following is a dialogue with a critic and a broker, demonstrating Negative Inquiry.

Bill has received a phone call from his best client, Gary. Bill uses Negative Inquiry as a way of listening to Gary's complaints and helping Gary identify Bill's behavior:

GARY: Bill, this is Gary. I've called to let you know that I am thinking of changing my account to another broker. The rate of interest I am getting with my investments is much lower than I had hoped, and I have a friend in another company who can get me a much better rate for my money.

BILL: Gary, I sure would hate to lose your account. You're saying that you can get a better rate with a friend someplace else. (PARAPHRASE) Is the lower rate the only reason you are changing the account?

G: You're only getting me 5.9 percent; my friend can get me 12 percent. That's a big difference.

B: You're right, I can see why you would be upset. (FOGGING/PARAPHRASE) Is there anything besides the low rates that is causing you to want to change, anything that I am doing? (NEGATIVE INQUIRY)

G: Yeah, I'm afraid there is. You come to see me once a year to talk over my accounts. When you do that, you talk 90 percent of the time. I can hardly get a word in sideways. I have been wanting to tell you to change my portfolio to more risky but higher-yielding stocks, but I couldn't get you to listen to me. So when my friend, who listened to me, offered a better rate, I took it.

B: It sounds like I needed to listen more and talk less. (PARAPHRASE)

G: It would have saved you a client. I'm sorry, Gary, but I'm making the shift. By the way, if you had listened to me before like you just did, we may not have had this problem.

B: I regret what happened, Gary, but I am grateful for your feedback. It will help me be more sensitive to my other clients.

The difficulty with most lost clients is that not only did they lose a client, but they also did not learn anything. At least Bill, in the illustration above, learned about his own inappropriate behavior and now could begin to rectify some of the problems he had discovered.

MANAGING THE CRITIC

Negative Inquiry allows you a sense of control while being criticized. Usually, our emotions fire off, and we want to run, avoid, deny, or defend. This skill gives you another set of behaviors.

This does not mean that we won't still feel some anxiety, or even anger, at the critic. It just means that we will have some options while we feel that way.

My own experience has taught me that once the skill is integrated into your behavior, you also will feel much less anxious when under attack. You won't be so easily backed into a corner, with no place to go except to become defensive.

If your critics can get you on the defensive, you are much more open to being manipulated, because they will be directing the conversation, and you will be reactive. So Negative Inquiry allows you to defuse much of a critic's anger, while learning something about yourself, and the critic feels as if he or she is being heard.

A $10,000 LESSON

I once set up a series of training events with a particular denomination that had scheduled five two-week events from coast to coast. Since I have experience in working with many denominations within the Christian faith, it was not unusual to get such a contract.

I went to the first introductory workshop to acquaint the one hundred or so people who came to that event, with the basic ideas of Calling and Caring Ministries. The event went well. Lots of enthusiastic people at the end, and many people eager to attend.

After the workshop, I met with a large committee who was managing the event. I was assured that it would go. I left feeling confident. Two weeks later I got a letter stating that the first two weeks were canceled. There was no reason why. Only a brief note stated that they could not do the events.

I had gotten word of the cancellation from my secretary. I waited until I got home to call the client back. The following dialogue took place between me and the client. It was a time when I used this skill to turn my critic into my teacher:

JOHN: Bill, I received your letter notifying me that you had canceled the two weeks of training I had scheduled with you. Do you have some time now to talk with me about what caused the cancellation?

BILL: Sure, I have time to talk.

J: When I left you and the committee, it seemed that everything was OK and the training was a go. Can you tell me what happened that allowed the event to be canceled?

B: You charge too much for your training.

J: It is true that I charge for my services. (FOGGING) What made the amount too much?

B: When I went to get the task force together to talk about the funding, the different groups said they couldn't come up with the funds.

J: So you are saying that one of the reasons was the groups' lack of financial support. (PARAPHRASE) Was there anything else that may have contributed to the cancellation? (NEGATIVE INQUIRY)

B: I did not get the support from the committee that I had hoped. Each group was to help advertise the program, and several of them backed out, so we didn't have enough support to get the people to come.

J: So, if I have it right, there was the money issue and the lack of advertising support that caused the cancellation. (PARA-PHRASE) I'm wondering if there is anything else. Maybe something that I did or my staff did that made it difficult for you to go on with the training. (NEGATIVE INQUIRY)

B: Well, now that you mention it, there was something you did that caused my people to be pretty upset.

J: What was it I did, Bill? It's important for me to know if my behavior caused the cancellation. (NEGATIVE INQUIRY)

B: You said, in one of the lectures, that if you take the Bible literally, then you will miss much of the truth, because the truth is hidden in the stories Jesus tells. My people are biblical literalists, and they don't believe that you believe in the Bible.

J: I did say that, Bill. (FOGGING) Are you saying that because I made that statement, the people assume I don't believe in the Bible, and that is why they don't want me to come? (NEGATIVE INQUIRY)

B: Yeah, that's the real reason.

J: Bill, I'm sorry if I offended any of your people. That was not my intention. Is there anything I can do to discuss my intention with them? (ATTEMPT AT RECONCILIATION)

B: No, John. It is clear that they do not want you here. I'm sorry.

J: Bill, I want to thank you for talking with me and giving me this feedback. I have four other contracts with your denomination, and I will change my language so that I am more clear and not offensive. You have helped me a great deal. Maybe some time in the future, we will be able to work with each other again. Thanks for your time.

Bill became my teacher in a most profound way. Had I not used Negative Inquiry to discover what it was about my behavior that caused the cancellation, I would have gone on to the next group, made the same mistake, and lost another opportunity to share my message, not to mention another contract.

Turning your critic into your teacher is not always an easy thing to do. But if you are open to hearing about yourself and the effect your behavior has on others, you will learn a great deal about yourself, and can then have the option of making changes, if you choose to do so. If you don't make changes, then you can count on getting the same response from others.

Behavior Description requires the listener to become an astute observer of the speaker's personal behavior. It is a low-frequency skill, in that it is not used as often as some of the other skills described in this book.

Definition: Behavior Description is describing another person's behavior, such as body movement, physical changes, tone of voice, and actual verbal quotes, without being judgmental or accusatory.

Purposes: Three uses will be explored in this chapter. We will examine each of them, so that you can learn this useful skill:
- It helps the *listener* distinguish between inference and behavior description.
- It coaches the *speaker* to identify behaviors, rather than inferring inner motives.
- It points out the *incongruities* in the speaker's behaviors.

BEHAVIOR DESCRIPTION

Describing another person's behavior without being judgmental or accusatory

DISTINGUISHING BETWEEN INFERENCE AND BEHAVIOR DESCRIPTION

The first use of this skill is the ability to differentiate between an inference and a behavior description. Since all behavior is potentially interpretive, the skill of describing behavior makes no interpretation or inference of any kind. It only observes the behavior, and then describes the observed behavior.

In the chapter on the Perception Check, I talked about inferring the emotions from another person's behavior. An inference is a guess about the other person's intentions or emotions. Behavior Description is just the opposite. There is no inference whatever when using this skill. On the contrary, Behavior Description describes only what you can see or hear. Following are some comparisons between these two concepts.

BEHAVIOR DESCRIPTIONS	INFERENCES
1. **Mary dropped the book on the desk and walked out of the room.**	*Mary was angry, and it became clear that she did not like me.*
2. **The wind was blowing, and the van was swaying back and forth as we drove down the highway.**	*The driver was anxious and didn't want to take me to the camp.*
3. **Richard's eyes were moist with tears as the group stood to sing the school's song. While others were singing, he remained quiet.**	*Richard was overcome with emotion.*

When making an inference, you presume to know the intention and motivation of the other person. A Behavior Description makes no judgments about any inner condition or attitude. It is a skill that simply describes what all who are present could observe and agree upon.

When you are listening to another, it is useful to know the difference between inference and behavior, so that you are not believing that your inferences equal truth. Thus, the first use of this skill is to make you, the listener, conscious of what you are doing during the listening process. Stay aware of whether you are inferring, or simply noting what the speaker is doing or saying.

HELPING THE SPEAKER IDENTIFY BEHAVIORS

The second use of this skill is to help the speaker identify the behavior that is in back of the inferences that are being made. First, this helps the listener learn what behaviors produced the inferences. Second, it allows the speakers to learn more specifically what helped them produce their particular interpretation (inference) from a given set of events. An illustration may help to make this more clear. (The words in italics are inferential.)

You are sitting with Susan in your office. She has come to see you after making an appointment, though she did not tell you what she wanted. The conversation goes something like this:

Susan says, "I'm glad you had time to see me, because *I think you are trying to get me fired.*"

"I'ts not clear to me. Help me understand what happened."

"Yesterday, when we were coming out of the meeting, I saw you standing with Jim Lord, *and I know that you were talking about me.* Within twenty minutes, Jim was in my office, saying that they were going to make some personnel changes, and he wanted me to know. *I'm certain that it was you who influenced him to have me removed me from my job.*

"What was it that I was doing that gave you that impression? Was it my talking with Jim?"

"Yes."

"What was there about my talking with him that led you to believe that I was talking about you?"

"When I walked by, I heard you say, 'Susan should know.'"

"You're right. I did mention your name, and I certainly am glad that you came in to talk with me. There are going to be some changes made within the next two weeks. I asked Jim if he would tell you about the changes, because we have decided to ask you to take the new position that will be developed as a result of the shifts. We were going to wait before we told you, because we needed to clarify the job description. I'm sorry you misinterpreted our intention. I hope this talk will help clarify what is going on."

By coaching Susan to identify the behavior from which she drew the inference, her boss could clarify the real issues and intentions. This rapidly clarified what was going on, and Susan now has to change her inference, which was bordering on paranoia.

Thus this second use of behavior description is useful for clarification, both for the speaker and for the listener.

POINTING OUT INCONGRUITIES

The third reason for using Behavior Description is to become aware of incongruities in the speaker's behavior and, on occasion, to point those behaviors out to the speaker. You will notice an incongruity when the voice, tone, and accompanying body language do not match. Following is a list of some incongruities you might note:

- While yelling, a person says, "I'm not angry."
- You sit back in your seat as you say, "I'm ready to leave."
- You see a person smile as he tells you about the death of a loved one.
- A friend sits on his hands as he says he is open to telling you something very important.
- Someone tells you, "Come here," while motioning to go away.
- A politician says that he will bring you the best educational system, while shaking his head no.

I was training an entire faculty on a college campus to listen to one another and to the students. During a demonstration interview, I asked one of the professors what he would like to talk about.

His opening statement was incongruent, when he said with a smile, "I just buried my mother last Wednesday."

My response was, "You're telling me that you buried your mother last Wednesday, and when you said that, I was aware that you smiled. I'm wondering if it isn't difficult to get in touch with the pain of losing your mother. Any chance I'm right?" (Three skills were used in my response: A Paraphrase, a Behavior Description—"I was aware that you smiled"— and a Perception Check).

He leaned forward, and the smile went away when he continued to talk about the experience.

PRACTICING THIS SKILL

There are several ways you can practice this skill in your daily life. First, start paying attention to the behaviors of others. Watch people in public places—that is, at restaurants, malls, clubs, churches, and at home. If you own a camcorder or movie camera, have your own behavior recorded, particularly if you are in front of groups or committees. You will get a different perspective on yourself if you can begin to see some of your own behaviors, and how people may interpret them. Watch television with a different eye, looking for incongruities in guests on some of the talk shows.

After some observations, you will begin to note more specifically the behaviors of others, and that can make you a more sensitive person.

When describing a behavior, you can use all three parts of the communication process: 1. Words; 2. Tone; and 3. Body Language.

Words are a direct quotation of what someone said. For example, in describing this behavior, say exactly what Jane said: Jane said, "I'm not going to the meeting, so don't pick me up."

Or it can be the *Tone* of voice. This is often more difficult, because our vocabulary is smaller for the tones people use. You may want to use musical language, if that is helpful, such as: "He spoke in a very *soft* voice. Yet you could hear what he said." Or, "Jack spoke *slowly*, and his *loud* voice could be heard at the back of the auditorium."

The third form, *Body Language,* describes the movements or physiological changes that are occurring. For example: "When Carl stood up, he looked toward the floor, then raised his right arm and grasped the cane. Slowly he walked to the doorway. He leaned over, turned the key, and unlocked the door. With his left hand on the doorknob, he twisted the knob, and the door opened."

A SHORT TEST

The following is a brief list of statements to see if you can identify the difference between a behavior description and an inference. The answers are at the end of this chapter.

Place an "I" in front of the statement if it is an inference; a "B" if it is a behavior description.

_____ 1. Larry sat still as Mary moved to the other end of the couch.
_____ 2. As Mary moved away, she knew that Larry would not want to talk with her.
_____ 3. Mary said, "I don't know what is upsetting you so. If you would talk with me, I think we could work it out."
_____ 4. Larry lowered his head and sighed a deep sigh.
_____ 5. He was certain that if he told Mary his problem, she would not understand.
_____ 6. Mary was very upset, but still wanted to hear what he had to say.
_____ 7. Larry said, "OK, I'll tell you, but I probably will pay a high price."
_____ 8. Mary sat back on the couch and replied, "I'll listen. OK?"
_____ 9. Larry did not believe what Mary said.
_____10. "It will be OK," Mary said, and she leaned toward him and took his hand.

If you will practice this skill over the next several months, you will find that you will be rewarded with special insights about how others communicate with you. It will also allow you to be more observant, and therefore more aware of what is being communicated to you and what you are communicating to others.

Answers to test:
1. B; 2. I; 3. B; 4. B; 5. I; 6. I; 7. B; 8. B;
9. I; 10. B

Part

2

HEARING THE STORY

Everyone tells stories—children, youth, and adults of all ages. Hidden inside those stories, like diamonds in the rough, are the deep truths of the unconscious. Storytelling is a form of self-disclosure. You cannot avoid telling your story. You can only try to make it abstract, in an attempt to hide the deeper struggles you are experiencing. Story listening is not just becoming aware of the language the speaker is using; it is also the process of observing, in detail, the body language, plus the tone of voice expressed in telling the story.

When you learn how to hear the deep structure of stories, you never can be quite the same again. You will be able to hear others' stories, and you can work more diligently on getting in touch with some insights about yourself.

This chapter is an attempt to share with you some insights about story listening and how to do it.

STORY LISTENING

Listening for the unconscious meaning in a person's story, told through themes and metaphors

FIRST, SOME BACKGROUND

The perception that led me to story listening first came to my attention in undergraduate school. I had taken a course in English literature and studied the use of metaphor and symbolism in poetry and the novel. Though I did well in the course, I did not apply what I learned to normal daily communication. I thought stories were events created by authors. It did not become apparent to me that those same ideas occur in common conversation.

Many years later, I spent a year of my internship at a mental-health hospital and learned to listen to children's stories.

"Children's stories" are called primary stories. This story type is quite easy to hear because it is not very abstract. The metaphors and themes of the story are easily picked up, and thus the listener can quickly gather a lot of information about the child's struggles.

Effective and caring parents want to know what is going on inside their child, so parents listen very carefully to the stories of their children. Simply read a child's story that he or she is writing for school, and you will discover some of the inner struggles with which the young person is trying to cope. Here is one brief story, told to us by the mother of a five-year-old.

The mother and her daughter were standing at the sink in their kitchen. The daughter was standing on a small stool rinsing the dishes her mother had washed.

The mother said, "Tell me a story," and her daughter responded by sharing this one-sentence story:

"There was once a little girl whose mother put her into the bathtub, and the water was so hot that it burned the little girl."

This is a story form we call an "I know someone who." The language projected the child's own problem into the problem of someone else. Her mother picked up not only the "I know someone who" concept, but also heard the theme, or metaphor, the little girl used—namely, "into the bathtub" and "hot water."

The mother responded by simply saying, "Is the rinse water too hot?"

And the little girl said, "It's burning my hands."

A child's stories are simpler to understand because the language has not been developed to the point of high abstraction. An adult tells stories far more obtuse in nature.

THE FUNCTION OF ABSTRACTION IN STORYTELLING

Our minds are marvelous, for the brain does everything it can to protect us from being emotionally injured. While it provides a barrier against harm, it also gives verbal and nonverbal clues to what is being hidden. The biblical image of "through a glass darkly" is an appropriate metaphor for these hidden clues. You know something is there, but you are not quite sure what.

The purpose of the abstract story is to protect the teller from becoming too exposed when the environment is threatening. Many times, our relationships do not provide the trust that is needed to divulge our deeper needs. In fact, you are rarely aware of the meaning of the story you are telling. The meaning is evoked as an unconscious activity.

There are, however, times when you are aware that, due to the nature of your relationship with the listener, you intentionally hide the meaning through some story form. These choices will become more apparent as you learn more about story listening in the sections that follow. You may become aware that a good story listener often will know more about the storytellers than the storytellers know about themselves.

You may have had the experience of visiting an elderly person who keeps telling you the same story again and again. If you listen carefully, you will discover that this commonly told event has important metaphors or themes. Through these themes, it is possible to discern the deeper truth.

LEVELS OF STORY LISTENING

Four levels can be noted by the listener when hearing a particular story. Though these levels are not neat and clean (stories often are told at many levels simultaneously), they can be identified by the particular kind of language the speaker is using:

1. Data back then
2. Feelings back then
3. Feelings now
4. Self-disclosure (or the moment of "Aha!")

The following paragraphs will explore each of these levels, so that you will be able to identify which level(s) the storyteller is using. Each level can be determined by the language used in communicating a particular event in the speaker's life.

LEVEL ONE: DATA BACK THEN   This story level has some very specific characteristics. First, listen to the opening phrases, or verbal stems. Comments, such as "When I was a kid, I . . ." or "Back when I was in . . . ," are common ways to start data-back-then stories. A more literary form would be, "Long ago and far away there lived in . . ." or "Once upon a time there was . . . ."

In a book on myths and legends, I discovered that every story but one had a data-back-then beginning. Here are some examples: "In the beginning of the reign of Zeus . . ." ("Prometheus the Firebringer," by W. M. L. Hutchinson); "It all happened long ago; so long that it has all grown dim" ("The Argonauts," by Charles Kingsley); "Once, in the old,

old times (for all the strange things which I tell you about happened long before anybody can remember), a fountain gushed out of a hillside, in the marvelous land of Greece" ("The Chimera," by Nathaniel Hawthorne). One other such data-back-then opening statement, "And it came to pass that everyone who ate the magic fruit grew fresh and young again, however old and weary he had been before," is from "The Apples of Youth," by E. M. Wilmot-Buxton.

Stories in the Bible also use this same form of storytelling. The opening of both the book of Genesis and the Gospel of John use "In the beginning . . . ." That's about as far back as you can go!

Both personal stories and literary tales develop the language of data-back-then stories. By listening to this communication form, it is possible to hear the clues at this level. The data-back-then story is loaded with data and factual information, and rarely contains any feeling or emotional words. You may also hear a high tone from the front of the facial mask.

The function of this story level is to put the story in a distant context. It is a way of guarding against current exposure, thus reducing the risk level. You will hear this level very often in settings where there is emotional distance in the relationship. It is frequently used in social conversation, when you share a part of your past, and other persons respond with something out of their background.

LEVEL TWO: FEELINGS BACK THEN   The structure for revealing feelings back then contains elements that are similar to clues for data back then, but an important ingredient is added—the "feeling" element. I do not imply that persons are always naming a feeling when telling their story, but I am saying that there are emotions in the voice, and these also are expressed in body language. Occasionally, a person will express a direct feeling. Someone might say, "I remember five years ago, when I was really angry at my boss. He didn't treat me as if I were a human being." The feelings are expressed in the past.

LEVEL THREE: FEELINGS NOW   When this level of story is told, it will become very clear to you, as the listener. You will be able to determine a number of obvious effects. The face will often flush, or at least you may see color change in the cheeks, nose, ears, and neck. You may observe that the voice—which, while portraying the data back, is in the upper frontal part of the mask of the face, gives way to a voice tone located in back of the nose, for the level of telling feelings back then. But at this third level, it ends up in the throat, where it is heavily laden with emotion. The eyes are often moist with tears, though they may not be running down the cheeks. Glistening eyes, reddened cheeks, and softer, deeper tones of voice will offer some clues that are usually present.

The story being told is usually more direct and the language less abstract. Since any of the five story types can be told at any of these three levels, the listener may discover that some stories are shared at a number of levels at the same time. This means that different levels can be incorporated into the same shared event, particularly if the story is of some length.

Level Four: Self-Disclosure   If the listener makes a check on the deeper meaning of a person's story, it is possible that the storyteller will become aware of the hidden meaning within his or her own story. This is what I call the moment of self-disclosure, the moment of "Aha!" It is when the speaker's personal insight snaps to consciousness.

When this insight occurs, there are usually two kinds of emotional reactions. The person may either cry or laugh, depending upon the type of story.

There is the possibility that a person may be trying to share a story of joy, rather than a painful one. I have found that people are more likely to share their painful stories than their joyous ones, because stories of joy may be perceived by you, the listener, as if the storyteller were either crazy or a sinner.

The function of the fourth level is to bring to conscious awareness the meaning of our own story. Since the story is a type of container that holds deep meaning, and because our stories are expressions of our own inner mysteries, it is helpful to bring those to awareness. When we are in the act of discovering our own perplexity, life takes on greater meaning and understanding. When we bring our own pain or joy to consciousness, we have a better chance of working on it, getting resolution on those structures that make our life fragmented and dysfunctional.

One other benefit accrues in this revelatory act of being aware of our own story. It brings enhancement and richer hues to our relationships with others. It also gives us a different perspective, not only on our own life but on others. We soon come to realize that others communicate to us through their stories, just as we communicate to others through ours.

But these four levels of story become a more useful listening tool when you understand the types of stories that people are telling you.

TYPES OF STORIES

I can identify five types of stories that adults tell when sharing with another person part of their own life journey. These types are not formal, nor are they conscious to the storyteller. The unconscious mind is sending forth the clues. The types of stories can be told at any of the four levels mentioned above. Frequently, a story is told at multilevels and can incorporate several different story types, all at the same time. The discussion below will elaborate on the different types. The following are the most common and frequently used story forms.

A REINVESTMENT STORY   A Reinvestment Story is a story in which you, the teller, share how you have invested in something new by placing your time, energy, and money into the new activity. This story type is told when someone has begun to invest in other pursuits and is letting go of commitments that were made in the past. The reinvestment is the replacement of activities that are substituting for long-term committed behaviors and undertakings. Several examples might help clarify this type of story.

You are sitting with a church member who previously was very active. You have made an appointment to meet with this member in a nice restaurant for lunch. Nancy is age thirty-eight, a person you have known for several years. She has taken seriously her church work and, in the past, has been active in the choir, taught on occasion in the religious education class, and was regular at church. However, she is no longer active. The reinvestment story she is about to tell you might sound something like this:

"You know, I used to be pretty active in the church, but for some reason, I have just gotten out of the habit. About a year ago, I started to work as a volunteer at the local fire station, and I have ended up as the dispatcher on Sunday morning. It's kind of funny, because I used to feel really close to the people at church, but I seem to have more friends now at Local Station Number 5."

It should be fairly clear that this story tells you about the reinvestment that has taken place between the once-invested church activities and those now involved in her volunteer work. You will recognize that this story is heard when a person is deinvesting in a bonded relationship.

This follows the stage of giving up on the relationship and sealing off the pain associated with it. This type of story occurs as a result of the sealing off of the emotions, and it tells the listener that there may be unresolved grief and loss still in the unconscious mind.

I do not wish to imply that such reinvestment deals only with religious institutions. Reinvestment stories can and do refer to matters beyond these groups. A marriage that is beginning to fall apart often reveals some of the same clues. The wife who keeps spending more and more time at the church or club, and less and less time with her mate is often experiencing the same emotions as one who is leaving a group.

The reinvestment story is a mildly abstract form of telling you that the bonding which the person once had is now changing, and that the change is a type of loss or grief. It is revealing to check out what is behind that reinvestment. Skillful listening is very useful in finding the hidden meaning.

Read aloud the following story, based on the reinvestment of the woman mentioned above, and see if you can become aware of its deeper meaning.

Nancy says to you, "I really was active in the church for quite a while. It was a very important part of my life. My family had been active in the church, and I naturally came to enjoy my work there. I was the pianist for Sunday school for many years, and I always enjoyed that. One Sunday morning during the pastor's sermon, he put women down as some kind of second-grade citizens, and I resented it terribly.

"It just so happened that, the following Monday at work, a friend asked if I would be interested in helping her for a weekend at the firehouse, because they were short one person. She said I would only need to be there for one day. I went, and the people were really nice to me, and I felt that my services were useful and wanted. Over the next several weeks, I went back to the fire station with my friend, and now am a full member of the force and love it. It's not that I don't believe in God. I do. But I have discovered that I don't need to be scolded about who I am. Anyway, I am having a great time with my new friends."

This reinvestment story contains many meta-stories—that is, a story hidden inside a story. The word *meta* means inside of, or alongside of.

Imagine that Nancy is talking to you. What do you believe the messages are to you, the listener? Make a guess at what you think they are. Either jot them down or just keep them in your head, and see if you can identify the deeper issues.

Through this story, you should be able to hear some of the following issues: (1) Nancy has replaced the church with her commitment to the fire station. (2) When she lost the relationship with the church, pain resulted. She does not say anything about that pain directly, but you can make a guess that there is still pain within her concerning her relationship with the pastor. (3) The inclusion of the new friends at the firehouse, and the absence of any mention of the church friends, is a way of saying that she misses her church friends, but the unconscious mind suppresses any direct mention of them, except by producing the polarity of their absence.

The reinvestment story is, therefore, an important story structure, because it almost always contains predictable elements. These elements, or themes, may include loss (due to the change in one's invested association with one set of relationships to a newly bonded affiliation).

Another theme is that of rejection, perceived in several ways. The statement about the pastor, and an inferred rejection of friends at the church, who apparently did not respond by following up on her when she no longer attended the church, are two such possibilities.

Still a third or fourth might be that of transition. (We will discuss later a story form called "transition.") Transitions have three stages: an ending, a stage of confusion, and a new beginning. When someone goes through a process of reinvestment, the story has close parallels to that of transition, because the person is moving from the ending of one relationship to the beginning of another.

One of the difficulties of such changes is that these are not clean endings. The person reinvests in the new relationship without ending the old. This means that leftover feelings and incomplete endings are taken into the new relationship. Usually, sometime in the future, those feelings will return to consciousness at some inappropriate time. The person may become inappropriately angry at some small event in the new relationship. Often, that behavior is misinterpreted and adds to the confusion of the storyteller.

Behind the reinvestment story are many issues. It is frequently helpful to check out what is hidden within those stories, so that the individual can achieve closure on endings, or open the possibility of returning to the old relationship.

THE REHEARSAL STORY   In the rehearsal story, the individual tells a story out of the past. Through hearing it, the listener can become aware that the event retold contains the same themes as the current problems facing the person. When the person rehearses (tells the story or theme again), the listener is able to hear common themes through the use of metaphors, single words, phrases, or complete thoughts.

I overheard a marvelous rehearsal story from a pastor who was chatting with other church leaders while we were standing in a hallway on a break. The pastor mentioned that he had just visited a parishioner and was told a significant rehearsal story. The church member was in the hospital, seriously ill with cancer. The patient asked the pastor if he had any large trees in his backyard.

The pastor responded that he did, but then did an important thing. He turned the story back to the storyteller. The pastor did not get hooked into telling his own story, but listened to the other person instead.

He asked, "Do you have large trees in your backyard?" The parishioner responded that he did, and then told this brief story. "As a matter of fact, I have one that is a beautiful old tree, but it is rotting out on the inside, and I think it is going to die, so I guess I had better cut it down."

The pastor heard the deeper story by picking out the metaphor and used it as part of the feedback for the story check. His response was, "I'm wondering if, when you find yourself in the hospital, you don't feel like a tree that is rotting out inside, and if maybe you feel that life is cutting you down. Any chance that this is what you are seeing happening to yourself?"

In listening to a rehearsal story, you become aware of the power of the spoken word. Verbal expressions convey more than you may think, because the mind creates metaphoric representations, which are saying more than what is said on the surface.

For example, as I am writing the opening sentence of this paragraph, I am interrupted by the person sitting next to me on the airplane. I am on my way from Columbus, Ohio, to San Antonio, Texas, via Atlanta. The woman seated next to me asks if her granddaughter could sit and watch me type on my portable word processor, because she loves to read, and she has just completed first grade.

"That would be fine," I say.

I stop typing for a few minutes, start to talk with the child, and an idea emerges. I could get her to tell me a story. I know that children love to tell stories, and within those stories there could be deeper issues about the child that I could discover. I tell this little girl, Lauren, that if she will tell me a story, I will type it into my computer, and she can watch me. She says that she would like to do that. Little children are delightful, because they have not stopped learning yet. Many adults, I think, have stopped exploring, have stopped investigating the depth and breadth of life.

So I asked her to tell me a story. And this is how the story and conversation develop:

"Books are fun to read. I have read a lot of them. I have more fun with my friends. I have one named Amy. She likes to read books too. My favorite book is my bunny book. I like it because I like bunnies. They are pretty. The bunny doesn't say anything . . . it just runs away." (Have you ever felt like a bunny that wanted to run away? What is it like when you want to run away? Is it sad?) "Yes." (Tears come to her eyes.) (What happened to the bunny when it ran away?) "It hid in the ground. . . . Grandma Bishop had one that hid under a woodpile." (Why did the bunny run away?) "He was afraid that someone might shoot him." (When you want to run away, do you get frightened too?) "Yes."

As a child can tell a story with its meaningful metaphors and themes, so can an adult, particularly an older adult. I recall an experience with my father. At the age of eighty-nine (two years before his death), he fell and broke his hip. I was called by my oldest sister, who informed me of his accident, and she asked me if I would go to see him at the Elks National Retirement Home in Bedford, Virginia. I assured her that I would, and I flew down several days later.

When I walked into my dad's hospital room, he was sitting in a chair, tied with a towel so that he would not slip out. He was sitting up for the first time after a pin had been placed in his hip. His glasses were off, his hearing aid was out, and his teeth were sitting in a glass of water. All these cyborg parts were sitting on the dresser.

I knelt down on the floor in front of him, so that he could see and hear me. I said, "Hi, Dad. How are you?"

Rather than saying how badly he felt, or some such response, he told me two brief rehearsal stories at the data-back-then level. The farther back a story starts, the deeper the pain it represents.

My dad said, "Did I ever tell you that when I was seventeen, I worked for the Pennsylvania Railroad? I was a telegraph operator then. You know, the railroads were really strong back then; they're darn near bankrupt now."

He immediately went into the next story, which carried the same themes, but had different metaphors: "Did you know that I worked for Bethlehem Steel in Pottstown for forty years? I built the towers for the Golden Gate Bridge. You know, someone just told me that they closed up that plant. It's gone out of business."

If you have an understanding of story listening, you probably will know what my father was trying to tell me—that is, what the meta-story would be. My father did not know, at the conscious level, why he was telling me these stories. He was not aware of the deeper message until it was pointed out to him. This is true with most of us. It happens because storytelling is the unconscious speaking.

As my father told me the stories, I heard their deeper meaning. I was hesitant at first to check out my hunch, for his loss is linked eventually to mine. I then took the risk and made the guess.

I said, "Dad, I'm wondering if you're giving up. Is this true?" His body immediately responded to the check. Whenever you get close to, or directly name the meta-story, there inevitably will be a significantly rapid change in body language. When insights come to individuals, there usually is a response of tears or laughter.

My dad immediately reached out, put his arms around me, and pulled me close to him. I put my head on his lap, and he put his head on mine and began to cry. It was only the second time in my life that I had ever known my dad to cry.

He cried briefly, and then was able to talk to me about what the story check meant. He was afraid that he was going to die.

The stories my father shared have obvious metaphors. In the first story, his reference to his age of seventeen put the story back in the past. (The level is defined by data back then.) And he told it again (rehearsal type story). I had heard the railroad story many times before, so the content was not new, just the setting. The story must always be interpreted within the context in which it is told. The same story told in a different setting may reveal a different meaning of the metaphors or themes.

In the Gospel of Matthew, many of Jesus' sayings are placed in a section called the Sermon on the Mount (Matt. 5–7). Most of those same sayings are also quoted by Luke, but the story is in a different setting, on a plain. When it is in a different context, the meaning of the metaphors most likely will be different.

Most often, the metaphors employed are referents to the storyteller. In the case of my dad's story, the railroads and Bethlehem Steel are symbols for my dad. Since these institutions were going out of business (a

common theme of both stories) it became easier to guess the deeper significance of what was going on with my father. Such symbolic language
is a creation of the unconscious, and is very important when trying to
understand the deeper meaning of the story.

Listening to a Pastor's Stories

One of the most fascinating aspects of story listening is the ability to
hear what your pastor (or any other speaker) is saying when delivering
a message. Preaching, in particular, provides a setting in which the listener can practice excellent story listening. If the listener were to copy
down the most commonly used single words, phrases, or stories, plus
becoming aware of metaphors the preacher uses, it would not take long
to discover some of the deeper struggles the pastor is experiencing in
his/her personal life. Remember, you cannot avoid telling your story.
The only thing you can do is make the story more abstract, or, if you are
a preacher, more theological.

While I was working with a group in a training event, one of the
members, the associate pastor, would be preaching at the Sunday morning worship service. We were holding the event in his facility, and the
group was planning to attend the worship hour. I was standing in the
church foyer when the associate pastor saw me, and he asked if we were
still going to have lunch together after church. I assured him that I was
planning on that.

He said, "Just listen to my first story, and you will know why I want
to talk to you."

This man was a sharp student of story listening and was aware of his
own story and its meaning. I listened intently to his first story, because
the first story contains the themes of all of the rest of the stories, except
that those themes will be in high abstraction. His first story, which follows, was a rehearsal story, at the data-back-then level. What would you
say to him if you were going to have lunch with him?

"Good morning, friends! I want to start by telling you a story
that happened to my wife and me this past summer. We had the
experience of going white water rafting down the Allegheny River
in Pennsylvania. Before we took our trip, we were given instructions on how to manage our two-person rubber raft in the turbulent water. First, we were told that there were two kinds of rocks
that produce the turbulent water. The small rocks produce churn-

ing water. Another type are the very large rocks which create large waves. We were told that when we came to a large wave, we were to lean into it, because if we didn't, the wave would flip us out of the boat. My wife refused to lean toward the wave, and she was flipped out of the boat into the water."

This story is an excellent example of how the unconscious produces themes and metaphors to communicate what is happening to the storyteller.

The following represents a list of some of his metaphors and their possible referents: river=life; white water river=turbulent life; two-person rubber raft=marriage; rocks=several causes of problems; flipped out of rubber raft=separation or divorce. Please note that the inference about the meaning of any metaphor or theme is only an educated guess. All metaphors have more than one referent, or more than one meaning. Many times I am wrong, but it does not harm the relationship if your guess is in tentative language, for this will help the speaker identify alternative meanings.

We sat down to lunch in a small restaurant just down the street from the church. He looked at me, his face lightly flushed, and said, "Did you hear my story?"

I said, "Yes, I think so, but I'm not quite sure what is happening. It sounds as if your marriage might be on the rocks. Are you separated, or going through a divorce?"

The pastor said, "My wife is leaving me next Wednesday." The two of us sat for the next hour, talking about his problem and what he was planning to do.

If you work at learning how to hear stories, you will enhance your communication with another in a very profound way. The rehearsal story is a form that everyone uses, because they are trying to deal with the pain that is residing in the unconscious. It is quite possible to bring these stories to consciousness and work on them appropriately. Listen to your own stories. Become aware of events you keep repeating over and over. Jot down some of the metaphors or repeated words, and you will get a new insight into your own life.

AN "I KNOW SOMEONE WHO" STORY   This is a story told through projection. The mind places on another person or thing its own problem or inner condition. The story form allows the storytellers to inform you about themselves by telling about another.

One of the ways you know you are beginning to hear an "I know someone who" story is that there are particular language stems (be-ginning phrases) which set this story type apart: "I have this friend who . . ."; "I know this pastor that . . ."; "I have this neighbor who . . ."; or "I go to this church that . . . ." The persons project their own deeper issues into the story about someone else, or some object.

The function of the projection is to protect the storyteller from being exposed while still dealing with the problem. In that sense, the story has a particular form of abstraction. The person talked about is often the person who is talking. Consider a funny little story I heard from an associate pastor as he began his sermon. The senior pastor, a trained listener, was sitting on the platform. The associate probably did not realize what he had just said to his congregation:

"I want to talk with you about two biblical characters, Peter and Andrew. Andrew was Peter's brother. Andrew did all the hard work, and Peter got all the credit."

It took all my discipline not to laugh out loud at this stunning example. There was not a ripple in the congregation, because the people were taking the story literally; they thought he was talking about Peter and Andrew. Surely he was talking about them, but he also was talking about himself through them.

The identified person, Andrew, becomes a metaphor, or representation for the speaker. Namely, Andrew=the associate pastor, and Peter=the senior pastor. He is trying to tell the congregation that he works hard and that the senior pastor seems to get all the credit.

A variation on this "I know someone who" theme allows the story-teller to project the inner state onto an object or institution. This deviation of the story type occurs when the individual assigns an object the characteristics of a person. It is a form of animation, the turning of an object into a person or animal.

Many years ago, I was ending a training event and had to stay overnight before catching a plane the next morning. During my wait, one of the participants asked if he could talk with me, and I agreed. We sat down at a table, and he began to tell me a story about his two churches. He said that they were schizophrenic because they were fighting with each other and with him.

For over an hour, he told me different incidents that had happened. I became aware that in most of his brief stories, the word *schizophrenic* was injected. That repeated word got my attention, and I logged it away with his other words such as "sick," "don't know what to do," and "fighting."

As he ended his story, I decided to check out what I had heard, and I said, "I am wondering if you're not afraid that you might become schizophrenic?"

He put his head down on his arms. In a few moments he raised his head and said, "Last week my father was diagnosed as a schizophrenic in a mental hospital, and I'm afraid I'm going to become one too." The designation of the church appeared to be a referent to the storyteller.

The Tree Equals Me

When you become aware of the "I know someone who" story, you will become conscious that you often tell such stories to other people. I have become conscious of my own stories, and even of the thoughts I have that I never say out loud.

My wife and I had a disagreement prior to going on one of our daily walks. As a result, we spoke very little during the forty-minute stroll. Normally, we would talk about many things, but quietness prevailed. When we came to a small tree growing along the sidewalk, I noticed that its leaves were brown and it looked like it was dying. I said to myself, "If that tree doesn't get some water, it's going to die."

As soon as I said that to myself, I realized what my own meta-story meant. The tree, of course, represented me, and the water represented the nurture and love that I need to receive from my wife. Within a few hours after the walk, we had worked out our problem, and the "tree" was green again.

Latent Language

Another way of talking about the "I know someone who" story is to refer to it as a story that uses latent language. Latent language is language behind a veil, the equivalent to the biblical image of "through a glass darkly." Its function is to maintain security while under a time of threat. The story is a "displacement." The speaker uses obscure ideas to represent inner struggles and concerns.

Usually, when people use a disguised form to tell about themselves, it is because they want to be safe from criticism or rejection. The more distant or abstract the referent person or object, the more need for personal safety. If you were listening to a person with very little trust in you, the language used would conceal the inner disturbance by representing it in things and other people. It also should be noted that the more mentally ill the individual, the more abstract the language. This is because healthy people have better coping methods and do not need to be so prone to denial in their language.

A man was sharing with his therapist the fact that he worked only two hours a day, that he thought he was unfit for work, and that when he worked he could not keep his food down. He then added, "Now take Germany. They are quite strict over there. They don't let people get by so slick. If people can't work, they dispose of a lot of them. They take them out into the field and shoot them." Within this brief story are two types of metaphors used within the latent language. "Germany," a very distant country from this man's reality, represents the foreign world of the therapist's office, and "people" is a mask for himself. The fact that people are punished or killed can begin to tell you how frightened this person was, and the necessity for hiding his deeper feelings by projecting this story into a foreign land and onto another person. The therapist in this setting carefully used language and metaphors that did not threaten the client (Vincent E. Maxxanti and Harold Bessell, *American Journal of Psychotherapy*, April 1956).

The story that I call "I know someone who" is one of the most obvious, but not always the one we are willing to check out. One of the difficulties we all have in story listening is that we tend to take the person literally. There are times when that is quite appropriate, but most of the time, a person is saying something much more significant.

AN ANNIVERSARY STORY   An anniversary story contains the themes of an event that happened in the past, but at the same time of year. The classic cultural event is known by those who become depressed at Christmastime, and do so every year.

You also may know of it around the death of those who die on the anniversary of the death of their mate, or that of some other important person in their life. The anniversary story is a type of rehearsal story, but the timing is crucial. You will often hear an anniversary story upon visiting a widow on the day before the first anniversary of her husband's death.

While sitting with her, she might tell this story: "I have really been sad lately. I have lost a lot of friends here at the nursing home. It is very hard to give up those you have learned to love."

Or the content may be more abstract, as you visit a friend who lost his wife a year ago. He tells you, "I sure don't know what is happening to our teenagers these days. The one next door took their six newborn kittens, put them in a burlap bag, and dropped them in the river. Isn't that the worst thing you ever heard?"

You could do a story check on the themes. It might sound something like this: "I'm wondering if, after losing your wife a year ago, it doesn't feel like being put in a burlap bag and drowned in the river. Has a big piece of you died also?"

Frequently, persons have no conscious awareness of the anniversary characteristics that are driving their emotions and behavior. Several weeks before writing this section, I was aware that I was very irritable, angry, and mildly depressed. Usually, I am a person of high energy, and I am not one to get depressed. This period of unsettled anxiety lasted a little over a week. I recall snapping at my wife, who, in turn, snapped back. In fact, we were both quite miserable.

One evening we went out to eat at a local cafeteria. As we were standing in line, I asked my wife what was bugging her. Within a few minutes, she turned to me and said that she had discovered what was going on. She pointed out that it was the seventeenth anniversary of her mother's death—June 10. When she spoke of it, an awareness came over me that June 8 was the eighteenth anniversary of my mother's death. As we were both able to talk about it, explore some of the emotion, and even cry a bit, the pain lifted, and within a few hours we were feeling normal again.

I became aware during this time that not only was I distressed and feeling sad about my own mother's death, but after eighteen years, I was still involved in doing so. That is what anniversary stories try to do. They rehearse the event at the same time of year and work through more of the emotions. The next time you have some "bad days," you might want to ask yourself, "What time of year is this? Did something of emotional significance happen at this time or near this date?"

I believe it is important to mention that when anniversaries do occur, not only are you working on the emotions evoked by the past anniversary event, but you are reworking other incomplete emotions that carry the same theme. For example, a loss occurs in your life, and you begin to reexperience it at anniversary time. When that occurs, you are working not only on that event, but on many other events that have the same characteristic motifs.

If you ever suffered the loss of a child, you know that on the anniversary of that death the occasion will act like a low-pressure weather system, which sucks in all other similar thematic unfinished griefs. That is why those events are so emotionally powerful. You are not dealing just with the central event, but with all those other times you avoided completing the grieving process. At that point, you are working on past events at the same time.

A TRANSITION STORY   The development of transitions is fully explored in the book *Managing Transitions: Making Sense of Life's Changes,* by Dr. William Bridges (Redding, Mass.: Addison-Wesley Publishing Co.). There are three stages for all transitions: endings, language indicating confusion (called the "neutral zone"), and beginnings. As I listen to these elements in stories, I am aware that many stories have one or more of these themes. When I check the stages, I find that these people are indeed going through some kind of significant change in their lives.

Most people do not have difficulty with change, but they do with transition. For example: an employee says, "I'm not sure that I want to be in this job any longer. I am getting bored, and I think I want to try something else. The difficulty is that I'm not sure what I want to do." This story contains elements of an ending and the entrance of the state of confusion.

I sat with a couple who were thinking of becoming less active in the life of their church. In exploring the issues in their lives, I found that both were entering into a state of inner change. They had been hurt by a lot of things that had been going on in their lives, both at work and in the church. The man said that he had made some suggestions at work to restructure the company, and was now working on those changes. He also tried to make some major changes in his church, but that did not work out as well. In fact, his suggestions were "shot down" by several people who resorted to public innuendos. The event pushed him over his emotional threshold, and he began to back up emotionally. He was entering into a stage we call the desert time—a time of releasing images and understanding. It is a time of loss of innocence, which means a considerable loss of inner belief systems.

His stories were very emotionally moving, even life changing. Because he was in a time of personal transition, his stories were filled with the themes of the shifting sands of his life. He was moving into a wilderness, a time of letting go and facing confusion.

When these transition stories become apparent, the listener's role is to provide the kind of support necessary for the person to remain in the desert, in order to accomplish what that stage can provide for the person.

Desert times are when you find a new vision for yourself. It is like having your life in dry dock for a while, where you can kick off all the barnacles that could get you into trouble later. There, one is allowed to sweep his or her house clean.

So far, we have been learning about the storyteller. Usually, that is not much of a learning curve, since everyone tells stories. The barrier to learning is the listener. The greatest difficulty in listening is what listeners will do with the emotions and information that come to their consciousness while other persons are telling their stories.

SUMMARY OF STORY TYPES

Five types of stories will be told frequently as you listen to other persons:

1. **Reinvestment stories** tell of shifting commitments and loyalties.
2. **Rehearsal stories** tell of events in your past life which you retell (rehearse) to inform the listener of what is going on now in your life.
3. **"I know someone who" stories** project your inner condition onto someone else or some object.
4. **Anniversary stories** are a type of rehearsal story told at a given time of the year, to deal with the unfinished pain or joy of that event.
5. **Transition stories** contain the themes of endings, confusion, and beginnings.

THE NATURE OF COUNTERSTORY

Counterstory is the story that comes to your consciousness when you hear the story of another person. Your mind picks up its themes at the unconscious level. Your mind then scans its own history and locks onto a similar story thematically, and the counterstory surfaces in your consciousness. The normal response is, "Yeah, I know what that's like. As a matter of fact, if you think you had it bad when you were a kid, you ought to hear what happened to me!"

Most of the time we tell our own story, and that might be acceptable in social conversation. However, when you want to deal with another person's story of deep pain, it is best not to tell yours, at least not yet, as the telling of it tends to shut down the other person's story. Refrain in particular if your story is a type of "can you top this" response.

One of God's greatest gifts is that of counterstory. Yet that gift can be one of your worst enemies, when it comes to listening. If you use the gift correctly, you will find that it can be used to the storyteller's benefit.

When the counterstory emerges into your consciousness, and sometimes it is only a vague awareness of something going on in you, try to identify what is happening, including naming the emotions. The counterstory emerging in you contains some of the same thematic material as that of the storyteller. If you can identify some of the themes in your own story, you will have a better chance of getting in touch with what is going on in the speaker.

When someone tells you a rehearsal story with data back then, there is a good chance that it will remind you of a story of your own at that same time in your life. As the storyteller moves to go deeper into the story, your own counterstory begins to fire off additional memories to your own consciousness.

There is another factor that is very important. It may be that you will not allow the counterstory to come to consciousness. If that occurs, there is a good chance that you may act on the emotion and change the subject, in order to protect yourself from experiencing the deeper pain in your own life.

Imagine that a person is sharing an "I know someone who . . ." story that triggers in you an automatic response, so that you are feeling very anxious and mildly uneasy in the presence of the speaker. Stay aware of that emotion, and let it bring to consciousness any pictures or words you might associate with it. There is a very good chance that some event out of your past will snap to consciousness. In that event, you will find that the themes will be like those of the speaker.

As you listen to others, you will become aware that you will not be able to listen very well to certain persons. One of the main reasons for this is that *you can enter the pain of another only at the level you can enter your own.*

Because most of us are generally uncomfortable with being in touch with our strong feelings, we avoid not only our own, but also those of other persons. Generally, we try to get people to be rational and logical, so that emotions do not become a part of the issue. However, all of us are emotional creatures, and God has made us that way. Using that emotion to benefit ourselves without overreacting to others is always tricky.

Though it seems a bit odd, when you listen to another person, the speaker who is triggering your counterstory actually becomes your therapist. This person is making you become aware of your own story, which apparently needs working on. In one sense, when you are a listener, you not only are helping the speaker, the speaker actually is helping you at the same time.

Counterstory becomes a problem for those who want to visit others in their churches or at work. Many persons in our society are in a lot of personal pain, and we tend not to want to visit them and hear their painful stories, because they fire off our own. It is this tendency to avoid inward examination that forms a barrier to listening evangelism. Although some say they do not want to be pushy about their faith, they are more than likely anxious about the counterstories that might be triggered.

One of the central stories of the Gospels is that of Jesus entering the garden of Gethsemene. At first glance, there is not much to the story itself, but the meta-story is very significant. In many ways, this story is the model for healthy spiritual and physical life. There is a type of strategy, which, when followed, can help the Christian, or anyone else find a deeper and more productive life.

Jesus took the disciples with him into the garden. The Gospel of Matthew says that he then took three of the twelve with him farther into the garden, where he left them, telling them to "watch and pray." Jesus then went to be alone, and there in the garden, he fell to the ground and prayed. (Luke adds to this story that Jesus perspired great drops of blood.) After a time, he returned to the disciples, only to find them sleeping. He exhorted them to stay awake, and again he left them and returned to a spot in the garden by himself. The story then adds that Jesus returned to the disciples a third time, only to find them asleep again. He was then captured by the Roman soldiers and taken away.

The meta-story, or deep-structure story, can be seen by the repetition of the story themes. It is told three times, not unlike a hymn when the singer sings a verse and returns each time to the same refrain. This repetitive theme has a deep message about pain in our lives.

If you are to know the power of new life (resurrection), of putting away the old and taking on the new, then it is necessary to enter the pain of your life, wrestle with it, and let it be your teacher. Jesus explicitly did not want to enter the pain of the cross. He asked God if there was any way out of "drinking the cup." The response was an implied "No." Thus the cross is one of the most important models of human life ever revealed. If you want to become well and be renewed, you must enter the pain of your life, not avoid it. Trusting that pain is always difficult. It always has been, and always will be. "Narrow is the gate and few there are that find it." Take up your cross and follow.

This model of life as struggle is represented by many other stories of the Old and New Testaments. When you enter your own pain, you will be like Jacob wrestling with the angel. When you come away from the event, you will have two things—a healed wound and a new name (identity).

As a caring listener, you not only will work hard at listening to another, but you will be in touch with yourself. By knowing something of your own story, you will be able to be present appropriately with those for whom you are caring.

THE SKILL OF SILENCE

All the skills mentioned above are called active listening skills, because they require the listener to interact with the speaker. Silence, however, is another skill that also is very important. Sometimes it is important to just be with the person, listen, and not give much feedback.

Silence is often difficult because we want to tell our own story. When persons are engaged in telling a particular event, let them spin it out. After the story is finished, you can then be more active with them. I am not saying that you should be silent all the time. The creative use of silence is more to the point. Knowing when to interact and when to keep silent is accomplished by much practice and by watching the response of the speaker. Remember that the response you get is a result of the message you sent.

MAKING A STORY CHECK

Checking out the themes and meta-stories is part of the skill of story listening. This is the process by which you make a guess at the meanings of the deeper-structured stories you are hearing. But first, you should ponder your relationship with the speaker. Checking out a story is done only after sufficient rapport and trust have been built. If you do a check without appropriate rapport, people may consider it an invasion of privacy and become resentful and emotionally distant from you. When you have built strength in the relationship, then the check is perceived as caring and helpful.

Here is what happened when a listener made a story check without first building rapport. He had finished his training on listening skills and was on his way home via airplane. He was seated by a man who began to tell him a story. At the end of the story, the listener made a story check. As a result, the man reached up and punched the button for the flight attendant. When the attendant came, he asked to be seated in some other seat, because he did not want to be seated next to this "psychic."

When enough trust has been built, you may find it appropriate to make the story check in order to be helpful to the speaker.

The story check is made up of three parts:

1. the stem,
2. the name of the meta-story (theme or metaphor), and
3. a question.

Stems consist of tentative language, which allows the listener to be only making a guess. After all, the feedback infers that the listener knows what is being said. Frequently I am wrong, but that has never been a negative. The speaker simply tells me I am not right, and goes on to tell me another story.

Language to make up the stem could be: "I'm not sure about what I just heard, but I would like to check something out with you"; "I'm wondering if . . ."; "It seems to me that . . . ." Tentative language always uses "I" for the subject of the inference, not "you" as a direct address.

The identification of the meta-story occurs after the stem is made. If the storyteller is using metaphors, then it is important to use the same metaphor or a simile in the story check. You may remember the story told earlier about the man who was dying of cancer. He told the story of the tree that was rotting out. With that story in mind, the meta-story check would sound something like this: "I'm wondering if right now you might not be feeling like a tree that is rotting out on the inside, and if that isn't pretty scary for you. Would that be true?"

Rather than use a metaphor in the story check, you may wish to point out a repetitive theme that has been noted. A theme can be detected by the recurring use of a single significant word or phrase.

There are times when the theme will consist of stories told to you several times. This repetition of events often occurs in older persons. The repetitive story is very significant because it represents the effort of the unconscious trying to work out some important issue.

One of the easiest ways to hear these repetitive themes is to hear a pastor preach over a series of weeks. By tracking language, either theo-logical or secular, you will be able to make a fairly accurate guess at what is going on inside the person's personal life.

Not long ago, I was presenting an introductory workshop on Calling and Caring Ministries with a group of church leaders. At the end of the event, one of the clergy approached me in a rather challenging way, questioning whether story listening could really be done, especially whether you could hear a pastor's themes in sermons. I told him that if he would send me three consecutive sermons, either written or on audio-tape, I would test the theory. Several weeks after I returned home, he sent me three written sermons that had been preached on Passion Sun-day, Palm Sunday, and Easter Sunday. I picked up the first sermon and read the first sentence: "When I was a little kid, I lived in a small town that had a grocery store that sat in a fork in the road."

After reading that, I made a note to myself about what I thought the rest of the themes in the sermon would be: "Fork in road equals decision time. Grocery store equals preacher sitting in the fork in the road."

In the second sermon, he told of Jesus in the garden of Gethsemene, making the most difficult choice of his life. Here the same theme appeared.

Some time later, I met this pastor, and in the conversation, he shared with me that at the time he had written those sermons, he was in the process of making one of the most difficult decisions he had ever had to make. It becomes quite apparent that you cannot avoid telling your story.

Story listening is the skill of listening to patterns of metaphors and story themes, which allows the listener to ascertain the deeper meaning of the painful event or story. The story is a container which holds the truth of the unconscious. By bringing the unknown story to conscious-ness, it is possible to work more effectively on its pain for the purpose of resolution.

This chapter supports the theory that language is a representational system of the unconscious. If a trained listener correctly uses the skills of story listening, it is possible to discover some of the dysfunctions that cause difficulty.

Story listening is not learned quickly. It takes many hours of practice, but I urge you to try it. It can change your life.

To understand story polarization listening, you must have read the previous material on story listening. In fact, it will not make much sense if you have not.

Story polarization listening helps you in becoming aware of the polarities, or the opposites, that occur within a person's story. I indicated in the story-listening chapter that you cannot avoid telling your own story. In this chapter, I will argue that you cannot avoid telling your story in polarities.

The creation of the polarities is not an intentional act of the conscious mind, but a way of indicating balance in the life of an individual. Thus, this chapter will explore the following concepts: (1) the nature and characteristics of a polarity; (2) the essence of balance; (3) how to interpret polarities after you hear them; (4) how to perform a perception and story check, based on the polarities that you have heard.

STORY POLARIZATION LISTENING

Listening and responding to the polarities (opposites) in a person's story

THE NATURE AND CHARACTERISTICS OF A POLARITY

The following biblical quotes will exhibit the nature and characteristics of a polarity. The most famous and obvious are found in Ecclesiastes 3:1-8:

A time to be born . . . . a time to die;
A time to plant . . . . a time to pluck up;
A time to kill . . . . a time to heal;
A time to break down . . . . a time to build up;
A time to weep . . . . a time to laugh;

A time to mourn . . . . a time to dance;
A time to cast away stones . . . . . a time to gather stones;
A time to embrace . . . . a time to refrain from embracing;
A time to seek . . . . a time to lose;
A time to keep . . . . a time to throw away;
A time to tear . . . . a time to sew;
A time to keep silence . . . . a time to speak;
A time to love . . . . a time to hate;
A time for war . . . . a time for peace.

From the New Testament, we also have verses that reveal polarities, such as this from Matthew 16:25: "For those who want to **save** their life will **lose** it, and those who **lose** their life for my sake will **find** it."

Or others that are more subtle:

And early in the morning he came walking toward them on the sea. But when the disciples saw him walking on the sea, they were terrified, saying, "It is a ghost!" And they **cried out in fear.** But immediately Jesus spoke to them and said, "Take heart, it is I; **do not be afraid.**"

Peter answered him, "Lord, if it is you, command me to come to you on the water." "He said, Come." So Peter got out of the boat, started walking on the water, and came toward Jesus. But when he noticed the strong wind, he became **frightened,** and beginning to sink, he cried out, "Lord, **save** me!" Jesus immediately reached out and caught him, saying to him, "You of little **faith,** why did you **doubt?**" (Matt 14:25-27)

A polarity is an opposite. The opposite may be spoken in direct juxtaposition—that is, "A time to be **born** . . . a time to **die.**"

Or it may be in a concept shared throughout the story, where the theme of the polarity is repeated two or more times, as are **faith** and **doubt** in the fourteenth chapter of Matthew.

In learning Story Polarity Listening, it is helpful to start with written stories, because it is possible to slow down the processing and look at specific forms of language. In the Ecclesiastes passage, the language is placed within rhythmic, closely associated patterns. This type of polarity is the easiest to recognize.

In normal conversation, those same characteristics (closely associated patterns) also may be spoken. You may hear it while visiting someone in the hospital:

LISTENER: Hi, how are you today?

PATIENT: Not so good; I was better yesterday.

L: What's different?

P: I'm starting to get depressed. I've never been depressed before.

L: Did something happen to make you feel sad?

P: When I first came into the hospital, my family came to see me almost every day; now they don't come anymore.

If the listener is aware of polarities, it will take very little attention to pick up this form of close proximity.

Your first task is to become aware of the polarity, because some form of polarity will occur in many of the stories you hear. What that polarity means is something we will discuss later in this chapter.

When the storytellers are revealing something about their life, the polarity may not be closely related in proximity of time, but it may be delayed in the story, so that the disparity between the two opposites is more abstract, and therefore more difficult to identify. It is quite possible that the polarity occurs in two opposing stories, told several days apart. However, most of the time, the contrasts you hear will occur within a specific story, or in back-to-back stories.

Thus the nature of a polarity is an opposite in language meaning, so that both sides (sometimes only one side is mentioned) are disclosed within a story or series of tales.

THE ESSENCE OF BALANCE

Listening to the polarities gives the listener a considerable amount of information that otherwise would be missed. The psychological balance, or the state of equilibrium, is preserved within a human being by a variety of internal parts which communicate with one another. These parts of our personality are there for a very specific purpose—to keep the individual in a state of equilibrium.

Our parts are often opposites in nature. For example, you will have a sad part and a joy part. You most likely have an active aggressive part and a lazy part. Each of these parts has a purpose. The aggressive part gets you going in the morning and protects you from being manipulated by those who would like to dominate your life. On the other hand, the lazy part allows you to slow down, so as not to burn out. If, however, one of these parts gets out of balance with the others, then dysfunction and maladjustments can occur. If you are overly aggressive all the time, you probably will lose some friends who find your behavior offensive. If you are acting on the lazy part much of the time, you will not accomplish anything worthwhile. But put the two together, and they tend to moderate each other, giving you an opportunity to do your work and rest.

Balance, therefore, is the ability to move freely from pole to pole with flexibility. Rigid behavior comes from the lack of emotional latitude available to move willfully between the emotional range that occurs between the poles.

In working with a middle-aged client in counseling, I discovered that she frequently avoided painful issues in her life. It is not that she could not acknowledge that they were there, but that she was treating the pain as if it were life threatening, when the circumstances surrounding the pain did not warrant the degree of her reaction.

After exploring some of these issues with her, it became apparent that her belief system had convinced her that if she went into her pain, she would stay there. It was useful for her to understand that her painful parts were purposeful, because they were her warning system that she might be getting into difficulty with some interpersonal relationship. Without too much work, she was able to develop a different way of responding to her polaric feelings. She thought she would not be considered stable if she were in touch with that pain.

She was able to perceive that life's polarities are used to give her elasticity between the outer edges of her life. These edges are the external boundaries of her consciousness.

A visual image may help. If this woman were to place on a sheet of paper, in circular form, all the polarities of her life, she would acknowledge the outer limits of who she was. For, in fact, she lives between these boundaries, which become the walls of her world.

I tried to help her understand that life is not the joy **or** the pain, but the joy **and** the pain. She was able to discover that she could move between the two with a comprehension that both emotions are her friends and allies. That is different from believing that joy is good and pain is bad. Both have a productive purpose.

This woman's belief systems around polarities is typical of most persons. We have not had much experience in exploring our polarities.

They represent our **assurance and uncertainty** about life. This mixed reaction leaves us unsettled and unsure.

Just consider the polarities of nature: cold-hot; light-dark; sunrise-sunset; clear-rainy; budding-wilting; sun-moon. The Old Testament tells us that God created the **earth** out of a **void**; that God makes the rain to fall on the **just** and on the **unjust**. In the New Testament, we are aware of contrasts: **death** and **resurrection**; **faith** and **doubt**; Christ **descending** into hell, then **rising** to heaven. Indeed, God has made a world of contrasts.

We are able to look through our telescopes at our own galaxy, and at others in the universe. Each of these galaxies, whether spiral, circular, or elongated in nature, has edges. Though they are millions of light years across, they still have boundaries, between which the stars, nebula, comets, quasars, black holes, and planets reside.

So too, the polarities of our life set up the configuration through which our life takes on form and structure. When our polarities are narrow and rigid, they affect our behavior and produce bigoted, intolerant attitudes and relationships. These attitudes are particularly harsh when we believe that we should stay on one side of the polarity without exploring the other. That would be "either/or" thinking.

When Elton Trueblood of Yokefellow Institute was nearing his eighty-fifth birthday, I asked him whether, as a result of his long productive life, he could say one word that would exemplify what he had learned in his Christian journey. He responded emphatically, with the word "AND."

I asked, "And?"

He responded, "Yes, and! Life is an 'and.' It is good and bad; it is made up of life and death; it is being close to God and sometimes distant. Life is an 'and.' It is the task of the Christian to live in the 'and,' in the ambivalence of life. When you have learned to live in the 'and' of life, you have learned to live."

Emotional balance is the quality of life by which each of us learns how to walk on a log in the water. Too much on one side, and you are all wet. As Jesus put it, "Do everything in moderation."

INTERPRETING POLARITIES

This section, and the one that follows, will help you understand some of the responses you can make, once you have heard the polarities.

A key to understanding and appropriate interpretation must start with the awareness of the polaric language described above. The listener is urged to listen for the polarity and its recurring pattern.

The following is a story with repetitive patterns of polarities. See if you can find them, and then make a guess regarding the inner struggle this person might be having.

When I was a child, I struggled to find what kinds of talents I had. It appeared that I could not do anything well. Some children could write well, but I could not. Others had very good social skills, but I was rarely invited to a party. I always seemed to be on the edge of the group, while others had the ability to be in the center of things.

Then I discovered that I could sing. That occurred in music class at school. But it also was discovered in church. I was asked to sing in the choir, and then was given solos to sing. As I entered my teenage years I found myself wanting to do well in sports, and I earned three letters in athletics, but I also was asked more and more to sing for different groups.

In my senior year in school, I was awarded the honor of representing my track team in the state final relays, but also was asked by the school's music director to be the only one from our school system to go to all-state chorus. I remember going to my track coach and telling him that I would be going to the all-state chorus. It so happened that both these events fell on the same day, and I had to decide which one I would attend. The coach became very angry at me and put my singing down, saying it was only for sissies.

I guess that part of my reason for going the musical route was that my track coach often demeaned me when I didn't do well, while my music director was more gentle and urged me to do better.

Now that I am an older adult, I never have regretted that decision. It has been my music that has helped me become the person I am today. It gave me inner strength and a positive self-image.

As a result of reading this story, you should be able to list many polarities. If you have a pencil or hi-lighter, go back over the story and underline the polarities. Give each one a number. You will note that some of them are very close in proximity, while others are far apart.

Here are some of the polarities I have identified; see if they match yours.

Identifying the Polarities

1. Young child . . . . Older adult
2. No talents . . . . Found talents
3. Others could write well . . . . . . Speaker could not
4. Others had good social skills . . . Speaker did not
5. Singing . . . . Sports
6. State track meet . . . . All-state chorus
7. School . . . . Church
8. Coach demeans . . . . Music teacher rewards
9. Poor self-image . . . . Positive self-image

Interpreting These Polarities   Several themes emerge from these polarities. One deals with that of personal identity—feeling good about one's self and feeling bad about who one is.

From these nine polarities, you now can begin to consider doing a perception check (see chapter on Perception Check). You may recall that in order to do a perception check, you must combine four components: A stem (tentative language); a feeling word (identify an emotion); a context; and a question (so that the person will respond to your guess).

As you look at the polarities you listed, or the ones that I have shared, ask yourself: "As the speaker is telling the story, what emotions do you believe he would be experiencing?"

Imagine for a moment that the storyteller is experiencing all these polarities at the same time. What range of feelings might he have at both the conscious and unconscious levels? Before you read on, make your own guesses, and jot them down on the edge of the page. You might want to list them on the page with the polarities.

When responding with a perception check, you normally would name only one emotion. However, when listening to polarities, it is appropriate to name two, if you choose to do so. Now let's proceed to name some of the emotional responses to the polarities in the story above.

A List of Emotions

Adequate . . . .
Inadequate . . . .
Lonely . . . .
Caught . . . .

Put Down . . . .
Angry . . . .
Satisfaction . . . .
Pleased . . . .
Accepted . . . .

You might be aware that many of these emotions are also polarities, such as adequate/inadequate, angry/pleased, accepted/lonely, and so on. It is therefore possible to either pick one of these emotions or pick one of the polarities of feelings.

An example of a perception check might be, "I'm wondering if you are quite pleased with all the things you accomplished when you were a teenager. Would that be correct?"

Or the check might include both sides of the polarity: "I have a hunch that you might be experiencing anger at your former coach for putting you down, while at the same time knowing the pleasure of going to all-state chorus. Any chance that you have mixed feelings about what is happening to you at the present time?"

STORY CHECK USING POLARITIES   You may remember from the story listening chapter that the story told is not just about events back in the past, but those "long ago and far away" themes have much to tell the listener about what is going on inside the storyteller at the present. The polarities carry repetitive themes that can be checked out in order to help the storyteller ascertain the deeper meaning of the message. Look at the polarities again.

1. Young child . . . . Older adult
2. No talents . . . . Found talents
3. Others could write well . . . . Speaker could not
4. Others had good social skills . . . . Speaker did not
5. Singing . . . . Sports
6. State track meet . . . . All-state chorus
7. School . . . . Church
8. Coach demeans . . . . Music teacher rewards
9. Poor self-image . . . . Positive self-image

To help clarify the deeper story, I shall refer to the above polarities—that is, (5) Singing/Sports. If we begin to group some of the polarities by theme, they could identify some of the speaker's deeper issues.

5. Singing . . . . Sports
6. State track meet . . . . All-state chorus
7. School . . . . Church
8. Coach demeans . . . . Music teacher rewards

Each of the polarities above has characteristics which inform the listener about times when difficult choices were made. Because these are themes that keep repeating, you, the listener, can begin to make guesses (inferences) about what those themes represent for the storyteller at the time they are being told.

The story check on the polarities above would sound something like this: "From what you have said, I have an impression that you might be trying to make some very difficult choices for your life. Any chance I might be correct?" (Overcoming poor self-image?)

Another theme that can be noted from the above story is that of polarities which represent the individual's struggle for personal identity. The telling of what others could accomplish, but the storyteller could not, is a repeated theme. The fact that these issues emerged in the story is not an accident. The storyteller's inner conflict over what he could or could not accomplish is part of the current struggle. The polarities below indicate some of these issues:

2. No talents . . . . Found talents
3. Others could write well . . . . Speaker could not
4. Others had good social skills . . . . Speaker did not
8. Coach demeans . . . . Music teacher rewards
9. Poor self-image . . . . Positive self-image

The story check on the meta-meaning (hidden meaning) could sound something like this: "You have told me that there were times in your life when you were aware that you did not do some things well, but that later you were able to accomplish some of these skills yourself. I'm wondering if there is anything happening now in your life that makes you feel there are some things that you are not doing well! Is there anything like that going on with you?"

There is no one way to do the story polarization check. However, it is important to make the guess in generalizations. That is, if you allow the feedback to come in a broad, rather than a specific reference, it allows a speaker's mind to search for themes at the unconscious level and snap them to consciousness.

It is then possible for speakers to become aware of the implications of their story at the polarity level, and consideration can take place regarding what the speakers may want to do as a result of the insight. The storytellers may wish to tell more about what is going on and explore any options they may have regarding their own self-image. They may also wish to go inside, to explore other times when they felt the same way. The listener's role is to help persons explore the implications of their acumen for their own general welfare.

The above illustration can help you understand the nature of the polarity and the methods of the perception and story check. You may wish to try several yourself, to see how you are doing in learning this skill.

POLARIZATION AS CONFLICTING PARTS

Each of us has within us parts of our personality that are in cooperation and conflict with each other. By definition, these parts make up many of our polarities. For example, I have many parts which produce many of the polarities in me. I have a professional up-front part that leads conferences and training events. But I also have a frightened little-boy part that likes to run and hide when it is confronted by anger. I have a loving part that is gentle and sensitive, but I also have an angry part that can be critical and domineering.

My father part is one through which I love my children, but my selfish part wants me to take care of only myself. The husband part wants to work out all problems that exist between my wife and myself, but my single-minded part avoids those struggles and wants me to go off and be alone.

Write some of your parts on a sheet of paper or on the edge of this page. (I use the word *parts* as a metaphor; I do not mean to imply that your unconscious is modeled after a machine with moving parts, or that the unconscious is a container with compartments.) As you write your list, be aware of the polarities that begin to show up.

When you become aware of the poles in your own story, it is because the different parts are sending different messages. Each part has a purpose, but the purposes frequently are diametrically opposed to each other. You may discover that your loving part and your angry part have difficulty getting along together, as do mine.

You may want to have these two parts talk to each other and find out what each wants from the other. In neuro-linguistic programming (see chapter on this subject), getting all the parts to communicate with one another is commonly called a parts party.

Emotional health is achieved when each of the parts is in communication with the others. This communication of talking to one's self is the way balance is created and a state of equilibrium is achieved. Often we discover that we are fighting within ourselves, a struggle we often call inner conflict. To reduce the inner disharmony, the parts need to discover their own interdependent function, and thus be of assistance to one another.

I am in San Antonio, Texas, writing this section of the book on a lap-top computer. I have been home only one evening and morning during the last week, and I will not be back for another five days. I will be at my residence for a day, and then will be gone again, training in Toronto, Canada. This training schedule of being on the road is exciting, rewarding, and lonely. A part of me enjoys immensely working with people from all kinds of backgrounds. But there is an element of me that fights with those parts and does not want to be on the road. My home part has the function of controlling the "want to be away" parts, attempting to keep the "away" portion of me in check, so that I am not apart from my wife more than necessary.

When my wife travels and trains with me, which she does much of the time, then the part that needs to be home is not very active, because my lonely part has its needs met, and I am content to be on the road for longer periods of time.

This is to say that my different parts attempt to keep me balanced. On occasion, my ego part, rewarded by the feedback I receive from training, starts to override some of the other parts and it gets out of balance. When that occurs, other parts kick in and try to right the situation. My guilt part says, "You are away too much, back up." My future-looking part tells me that I am not scheduling well, that I need to plan times to be in the office and at home.

It is as if these parts begin to gang up on my wanting-to-be-away part to get it back in sync with the rest of them, so that my schedule gets leveled out. But I can describe it another way.

Other parts of me also come into play, acting as counter balances.

These parts of my polarities represent much deeper polarities, and their implications begin to overlap into some of the other chapters of this book.

In the Life Commandments chapter, I talk about the deep inner-belief systems, which act as the infrastructure to our behavior. This private interior guidance system is often not in our awareness, but our beliefs shape who we are and what we can and cannot do.

I have become aware that each of my parts—your parts, too—has its own belief system, so that these components of belief are often in opposition to one another, or at least, are dissimilar, and seem to compete.

For example, my ego part believes that it has unending energy and can go on and on without rest. In contrast to this, my rational part believes that I am a highly limited person, and if I continue to overwork, I will burn out. These two belief systems are always at war within me. I am grateful that they are, because when both sides are pulling, they create harmony, equanimity, and unity.

Our deep internal beliefs are there for the purpose of providing the kind of flexibility that is needed for the variety of life events that come down upon us from time to time. Each of these parts and their beliefs give elasticity. Most of all, they give us alternatives.

I guess what I am trying to convey to you, the reader, is that I want you to become more and more aware of the great variety of beliefs and polarities which enrich your life, giving it meaning and versatility. If you will become aware of the different parts, you also will become aware that each of the parts has it own particular belief system. In many ways, a part is a sub-belief system. We often think of ourselves as having only one or two beliefs about a thing, when in reality, we have numerous ways of believing about a particular aspect of our life.

PURPOSE OF LISTENING TO POLARITIES

When you develop the skill of story polarity listening, you will be able to identify:

- many of the polarities in a person's story.
- some of the emotions that are communicated through the polarity.
- the characteristics of a missing polarity and its implications of the denial system a person is using.
- the language necessary to do a story check, using the polarities as a guide of the repetitive language.

- the belief systems of the polarity, and how that drives the behavior of the storyteller.

The purpose of all this is to help the speakers become more aware of their own struggles, and be able to facilitate alternative behaviors for their ongoing health. Through this skill, people are more capable of entering the clusters of events that often tend to immobilize their behavior.

Story polarization listening will take you some time to learn. Be patient, and it will not be as difficult as you might think. Start by reading short stories and picking up the polarities. Poems often provide a way of seeing the opposites that were going on in the author. Life is a series of polarities, a party of the parts. Don't let it discourage you—enjoy it.

ADVANCED LISTENING SKILLS FOR MINISTRY

Chapter

10

LIFE COMMAND- MENTS

Listening to the deep belief systems that drive a person's behavior

T he mind is capable of believing anything!

Life commandments are deep inner belief systems that act as the internal guidance gyros of your mind.

Just think, for a few moments, of all the different belief systems on our planet. Consider the incredible variations from one major culture to another!

I walked into a large Native American museum in Oklahoma. As I passed through the great vaulted foyer into the first of many large rooms, I walked up to a glass case in which there were a number of small shrunken human heads. The skin on the faces was like leather. The stringy hair was wrapped around the stands on which the heads were placed.

A small sign told about the heads. A young warrior, in order to be initiated into his village, was required to go to a neighboring tribe, capture one of the people, and cut off the head. He was then to shrink it, first removing the brain. When the head was correctly cured, it was presented to the tribe as evidence of the young warrior's manhood. The tribesman did this because he *believed* it was appropriate behavior.

During World War II, young Japanese pilots climbed into fighter planes, then took off and dove into American aircraft carriers. They believed that if they did so, they would be rewarded in Nirvana.

An Arab soldier, driving a truck filled with dynamite, drove it into an American barracks in Beirut, Lebanon, killing more than two hundred soldiers. He did so because he believed that his act would secure him the favor of Allah.

Christians, in the first century, allowed themselves to be eaten by lions or killed by the gladiators, because they believed they would be rewarded in heaven.

The human mind is capable of believing anything.

I was carrying my briefcase and luggage to the car on a college campus, when a woman who had been in my training event stopped me and asked if she could talk with me for a few moments. I agreed, and we sat on a bench outside the building. The following story was shared with me. It illustrates what the mind is capable of believing:

> When I was five years old, I remember that if I did not behave perfectly while eating supper, my father would send me to the basement and turn out the lights. Then my older brother would sneak down the stairs, grab hold of me, and scare me. He told me that over in the corner of the basement, where it was dark, was a big cesspool where the devil lived, and that the devil loved to eat little girls named Susan.

The problem was that she believed it, and forty years later, sitting on a bench next to me, she still believed it, except that it now had adult manifestations.

This woman told me that when she goes to church—and she never misses—she must say every word of every prayer, and she must sing every word of every hymn. She must be perfect in church, or she believes that she will go to hell.

Our deep internal belief systems ultimately affect our religious belief systems. That is what this chapter is all about. Why do we believe what we believe, about our world and about ourselves? How did we get our belief system? How do they affect our behavior? Is it possible to change a belief that has become dysfunctional, or sick? This section will try to answer some of these questions.

WAYS WE OBTAIN OUR BELIEF SYSTEM

THE EARLIEST LIFE COMMANDMENTS The earliest belief process occurs within the first year of life. These beliefs are learned at the kinesthetic level—that is, they are acquired through experience. They are not given orally. The child is too young to understand language, but can respond to tonal inflection. Erik Erikson's "trust vs. mistrust" is quite appropriate to describe what happens in this first stage of life. Can the infant trust the environment, or is life's situation too threatening?

What happens to a person's deep internal beliefs if, like one woman I know, the person is put in six foster homes in the first several years of life? Is it not obvious that the child will come to believe that no one wants her, that she is not lovable, that the world is a place of rejection, refusal, and disapproval? I know such a woman well. She came to me for therapy, and I saw her twice a week for nearly twelve years.

When I first met her, she was agoraphobic. At the age of forty-two, she was frightened to even go to her mailbox or walk a block away from her home. She believed that God was a vengeful, punitive God. She could not understand the concept of love, forgiveness, or compassion. Deeply internalized in her mind was a belief of distrust for the world around her. The only thing she could do was hide from it, staying inside the secure walls of her house.

The deepest belief systems are those learned in the first year of your life. Do you know what happened to you in that first year? You can never know it directly, but you can find out about it from members of your family. Ask them. You might be surprised what you can learn about yourself and why you currently believe what you do. My own personal journey may help to illustrate these early interpretations of the world.

I am the youngest of seven children. I was born in 1930, during the height of the depression. There were twelve of us: my parents, three brothers, three sisters, my grandmother Huber (mother's mother), and an aunt and uncle, all living under the same roof. Food was scarce. Dad, the only one working, brought home $7.50 a week to feed the whole family.

My oldest sister has told me that when my mother was pregnant with me, she had gone to church one Sunday morning to lead the church choir. While leading the choir, she went into labor. After church, she went to the hospital, but I was not born until the following Wednesday. A fascinating part of this story is that my grandmother had not known that my mother was pregnant, yet they lived in the same house. At birth, I weighed only a little over four pounds; my mother was a stocky woman, so she simply put on a larger dress, and no one was the wiser.

When my sister came home from church with the news, my grandmother began to cry and became quite angry. The tears occurred because my mother was having another baby during the Great Depression. The anger developed because my mother had not told her she was pregnant. According to my oldest sister, who was fourteen at the time, Grandmother scolded my mother severely when she brought me home from the hospital. The result of that interaction ultimately affected my own life and that of my siblings. Mother reacted by "overtaking" care of me, and my siblings felt it because Mother gave me so much of her attention.

The beliefs that resulted from this interaction may seem peculiar. I believed that I was an accident and not wanted, while my brothers and sisters believed that I was the favored child.

For many years of my adult life, I had to fight with the inner concept that I was not acceptable. This drove me to two sets of behaviors. First, it required that I had to prove my worth in some form. Second, it kept setting me up for failure, for when I would find success in some relationship or venture, I would then exhibit behaviors that made sure that success would not be accomplished.

Only after many years of hard work, and with the help of a therapist friend, was I able to begin to break that deep belief system about myself. In fact, this book is a result, in part, of breaking that inner life commandment.

Much of the hard work of being an adult is the reworking of our internal belief systems, so that they do not immobilize us later, in our ripening years. If this book does nothing but make you aware of some of your own life commandments that are getting you into trouble, it will be worth all my efforts.

VERBAL LIFE COMMANDMENTS   The second way we receive our life commandments is through verbal commands. These verbal commands may be given only once, or they may be repeated hundreds of times. When a child is told that he/she is stupid, dumb, or an idiot, and these words are repeated again and again, there is a very good chance that the receiver of these commands will begin to believe them and internalize them.

Since I was born during the depression, I have become aware of a whole series of life commandments from that era. One of those is very hard for me to break, even to this day: "Eat everything on your plate. Think of all those little boys and girls who will starve to death in China if you don't eat it all."

I often wondered how the food on my plate was going to get to China, at least without getting moldy. Other cultures have the same problem. Several years ago, in the *New Yorker,* I saw a cartoon of a Chinese mother, standing over her children seated around their table. She was saying, "Now children, be sure to eat all your rice, because in America, children have only junk food."

One of the most significant findings I have made is that many of the verbal life commandments are instilled during the ages of eight, nine, and ten. When I work with individuals who are manifesting dysfunction, and we begin to talk about their deep belief systems, we inevitably get back to a time in their life when they were vulnerable. It is during those latent years, when the mind is grasping to try to understand the world they live in, that children grasp at apparent truths and accept them into their inner world. Once these beliefs are anchored by reward, the belief becomes internalized, and a child accepts it as truth.

These truths support children's understanding of the world and who they are. The commandment is then lived out in varying ways.

For example, I interviewed a man who was on the edge of burnout. He was serving as a pastor in a twelve-hundred member church and found that this was quite a promotion for him, since he had come from a church of about seven hundred members. When he was in the smaller of the two churches, he was able to keep a commandment he had learned when he was a small child: "Be a good boy, and try to make everybody like you." Now the pastor is in a setting where he cannot make everyone happy. Thus, when someone from his congregation is angry at him because he is not a "good boy," he goes a little crazy inside, since he is not living up to the "law" of his life.

Unless he goes inside himself and begins to break that commandment by giving it up altogether, or at least by moderating it, he will push himself to his limits and burn out emotionally. That life commandment may have been attainable by a young boy in a small family, but it is quite impossible to keep with a large group of people. This particular commandment must be changed within him, or he will be in severe trouble.

I have seen careers destroyed because of dysfunctional belief systems. One pastor's credentials were revoked as a result of a belief system he was incapable of breaking.

This pastor had great potential. In a mid-life crisis, he left his career with a nonprofit organization and went to seminary as a means of entering the parish ministry. He graduated by the skin of his teeth, was approved by the judicatory officials in his denomination, and took a placement in his first church. During the first six months of his ministry, he did very well. He had the ability to relate well to teenagers, and his youth group grew dramatically.

Then something happened to him. He did some really odd things and got into trouble with his church leaders. For example, he forgot to take the offering three Sundays in a row. The treasurer was so angry that she refused to pay him for three months. He would set up meetings, and then cancel them just before time to meet. He would schedule some counseling with one of his parishioners, and then not show up. By the end of his first year, a church executive was called to remove him. He moved to another church, where the behavior was repeated. He moved again in his second, third, and fourth years.

I sat with him a number of years later, when he was in his ninth church in fifteen years. He had received a letter indicating that unless he changed his behavior, his ordination credentials would be revoked the following year. They were.

As I talked with him, I was able to get to the deeper belief systems that were causing the difficulty. When he was a little boy (age 9, he said) his parents told him that he wasn't as smart as his brothers and sisters, and probably would not amount to much. Then one day, a very significant thing happened to him. He believed it. And not only that—it worked for him. He began to do poorly in school, and that got him attention and pity from his parents. It worked for him as a child. But it became destructive as an adult. To put his life commandment in more formal language, it would sound like this: "You will never be successful."

The difficulty of believing this at a deep internalized level is that when excellent achievement is occurring, the emotion of guilt arises. Since he does not want to be a "bad boy" or a disobedient child, he acts in ways that ensure that he does not succeed. Knowing this man as I do, and attempting to help him break this life commandment, I think he most likely will keep it for the rest of his life, setting himself up time after time for failure, rather than going into the pain of the guilt and being disobedient to the commandment.

When I worked with him about breaking this inner law, his response was most interesting: "It is better to know that I can fail than to not know what will happen if I succeed."

During the time of struggle in this man's parishes, both of his parents died. I thought that then he might be able to abandon this old belief system, because his parents were not around to reinforce it. What happened was quite the opposite. He idealized his parents, stating that they were the perfect parents, and he could never disobey them. Now the commandment is even more anchored. The problem is not the actual parent, living or dead, but the parent in his head. The verbal commandments can be especially distressing when the individual has entered the second half of life and still relies on the belief system of the first half.

I became intensely aware of this as I entered my late forties and early fifties. One Christmas, my sister Doris, who is two and a half years older than I, came to spend the holidays with us. She brought with her a picture of my mother and father, with my sister and me seated at their feet. I was three and she was six. I had never seen the picture before. When I looked at it, I had a profound insight about a belief that I had carried for more than fifty years.

The picture was taken in 1933, in the heart of the depression. You will remember from a previous story that there were twelve of us living in the same house. Times were hard. The stress of trying to cope with a big family and the unending daily strains and tensions began to produce a belief in my mother, which she passed on to my sister and me: "You can never expect to be happy in this life." Then one day, we believed it. It has affected my sister dramatically and me considerably.

For years, I experienced moments of joy and happiness, but they were always accompanied by moderate to intense levels of guilt. It was as if there were a wall of emotion that emerged in me, so that it was not possible to encounter or engage the happiness and enjoy it fully. Because of the guilt, I would overreact to the events that were giving me a sense of well-being. If I was with a friend or a group of people, I found that I would interpret their behavior inappropriately, often becoming emotionally distant. They, in turn, reacted by making a critical comment, which would confirm my first awareness of the guilt—namely, that I should not be feeling so good.

All this was going on when I was unconscious of any understanding of life commandments or inner belief systems, long before I had the comprehension I have now.

With the help of a therapist, I was able to go back to that life commandment and modify it so it would be appropriate for my life at this time. I had to accept a new belief system—namely, that it is quite OK to feel a sense of goodness, success, and happiness.

The therapist told me to write a letter to my mother and tell her that her truth had become a lie, and I could no longer believe it. I cried as I wrote every line. How do you tell a mother who took such good care of you that you no longer believe her?

In retrospect, I have learned a great deal. First, I am now aware that when my mother died at the age of eighty-two, she no longer believed that commandment. In the last twenty years of her life, she obviously had broken it herself. That is one of the peculiar things I have noted. Those who often give us the life commandments do not believe them their whole lives, but change them to meet their needs at the time. However, *we* keep believing them as if they were eternal truths.

One view I now have of a life commandment is that it is transitory. It has its function and purpose at the time it is believed, but at a later time in life, it is possible for it to become inappropriate and even destructive.

These verbal commands are frequently given to us by persons of influence. They could be parents, siblings, teachers, preachers, members of our peer group, relatives, and so on.

When I was in tenth grade, my English teacher told me that I would never amount to anything academically. My problem—I believed her and became the class flunky.

Several months ago, I was rummaging through an old box and found my tenth-grade report card. In the first part of the year, I was doing well in English. By the end of the year, I was on the verge of flunking. I graduated with a class of ninety-nine students and was thirty-three from the bottom. No college would take me after high school because of my poor grades. If it weren't for the GI bill and the breaking of that commandment, I would not have the education I now have.

Later, I was invited to be the keynote speaker at a church conference. After the opening lecture, I came down from the podium and had started down the center aisle of the church when an older lady came walking toward me. There was my tenth-grade English teacher! She approached me and said, "John Savage, what ever turned you around?" My word, I thought, she even remembers how flunky I was thirty-five years ago. I responded to her question by simply saying, "God."

Here are some of the common verbal life commandments I have heard: "Be sure everybody likes you"; "If you take care of other people, they will take care of you"; "Don't ever let other people know how you feel"; "If you want to keep your husband happy, do whatever he asks." These verbal instructions may be appropriate when they are given, but they inevitably will get the adult into trouble later in life. They are frequently passed from one generation to another, and thus are what the Bible calls the sins of one generation visited upon the third and fourth.

Several years ago, I talked with a woman who needed the help of a therapist. Her problems were very severe, yet she would not seek help because of a life commandment that was told to her many times by her father: "Never tell what goes on in this family. We are a good Christian family." The father had raped this woman many, many times when she was a little girl. As an adult, she needed the best professional help possible, but she could not get it and still be obedient to the life command. She finally risked becoming disobedient and began to see a therapist.

In a training event, my wife and I were sitting with a woman who shared a command from her mother which served her well during her teenage years. The mother had told her numerous times, "You are the least sexy girl I have ever met. Stay that way." In exploring what this command had meant to her, she shared that it probably kept her from getting into sexual difficulty when she was a young teenager. However, it now had the effect of conditioning the way she dressed and the way she looked. She did not have a very good image of herself because she believed she was not attractive.

Most life commandments, when believed by the receiver, are useful for a particular purpose. When obeyed by the child, they are often functional in getting the child what he/she needs at that time. In one sense, each belief has a specific purpose and derives a particular reward for the believer. It is later in life, however, that those belief systems become inadequate for the tasks and relationships that are needed.

Part of my belief expression was to be passive, and in doing so, people would take care of me. I had the ability to hook people's guilt. This was done by a sad expression, a voice tone that was nonassertive, and language that was partially self-demeaning. Those behaviors came from a belief that I wasn't as good as my peers, and it certainly showed itself in high school, when most of my peers were in academic courses headed for college, while I was a shop boy, making blueprints and furniture. I do not imply that building furniture is a profession that does not take skill. It does. I am saying that I could not accept that, given the direction my friends were headed, leaving me behind.

Through a religious experience at the age of nineteen, I was able to change some of that belief system. I felt that if God loved me, maybe I could love myself. It was then that the earlier life commandment began to be modified. Later in my life, it became possible to show myself and others that I was not as dumb as I had earlier believed. It was possible to become successful academically.

The reworking or disobeying of a life commandment can virtually give you new life and purpose.

LIFE COMMANDMENTS BY INFERENCE   The life commandments most difficult to break are those that are learned through inference. An inference is an assumption you make about what another person meant, without checking it out for yourself. An example will help to make this clear.

A student in one of my training events, a young man in his late twenties, asked if he could talk with me for a few minutes after the event. He came to my motel room, and we talked for several hours about a life commandment he had discovered during the training. His story really intrigued me, as I had never heard one like it before. His ministry had just come to an end in his previous parish, at his request. After four years in his first church, he was aware that it was going well, that his parishioners liked him, and he them. Yet something was driving him to make a change. So, with the help of a denominational executive, he had found another congregation and moved.

He stated that he felt he had made a bad decision, that he should have stayed where he was. It did not take long for him to identify his commandment, which had been given by his mother: "Whatever decision you make, you will wish you had chosen the other." This became the driving force behind his move and the need to feel depressed, regardless of what he decided.

I asked him whether his mother was still living. He replied that she was, and I urged him to go to see her and check out what she meant by the commandment. He was resistant at first; after all, it is not easy to question parents about their intentions when you were a child. But with courage in hand, he confronted his mother.

Her response astounded him. When he asked her about the statement she had made, she replied that she thought it was a wonderful idea and that her mother had told it to her. She said, "If you make a wrong decision, you have other options."

He responded: "Is *that* what you meant!"

Now he has a problem. He had believed his own inference. Or, to put it more succinctly, he had accepted his own hallucination as if it were truth. He must now disobey the inference he had made. He must disobey himself.

Without a doubt, the most difficult life commandment to break is the one you have given yourself by assuming that you know what the giver of the commandment means.

I have noted that many deep belief systems are acquired through inference, through the behaviors of the commandment giver. Please be aware that these structures are transmitted without the giver's awareness. But the believer interprets the other's behavior as though it were intentional. This is how it works.

An older woman I will call Ruth came to see me over a period of a year. Most of the time, her husband came with her, because they were working on some of the same issues. That is, both were striving to break some dysfunctional life commandments that were erupting at the same time.

Ruth had grown up on a farm in a midwestern state. When she was on the tractor with her dad, he would complain about her mother, so the young girl became a confidant for the father. When she was working in the kitchen, her mother would complain about how insensitive her father was. Ruth was caught between her parents, not knowing which to believe, yet not wanting to believe either.

One day when she was eight years old, her mother told her that if she ever wanted to be happy in marriage, she should do whatever her husband asked and be obedient to his command. In the setting of ambivalence between her father and mother, Ruth chose to believe her mother. It solved the dilemma, and she became an obedient young girl.

On a neighboring farm, a young boy was being raised by parents with a different scenario. He noted that his parents, who often fought verbally, would stop when he tried to intervene. When he was nine, he believed that it was his task to keep his parents happy. Later on, in his teenage years, he was not able to keep the command because his parents divorced. He did not give up the command, however, but took it into his marriage.

It so happened that these two children, living on neighboring farms, later married. Their life commandments worked well for them in the first part of their marriage. She was obedient to his wants and did whatever he asked. He avoided all forms of conflict and did everything he could to keep peace in the house. They raised four fine children, had an excellent business which they ran together, were admired by the community, and life seemed stable and meaningful. Then at the age of fifty, something happened to Ruth.

One morning she awoke to find herself very dissatisfied with her life. The children were grown and out on their own. She found the work she was doing had become boring and meaningless. This gnawing, doubtful state continued for several months, as if she had been unplugged from life. She was still doing her daily duties and work, but she was hollow inside. When the inner vacuum reached high enough proportions that she became irritable and restless, she decided to do something about it. She notified her husband that she was leaving the business they had built together and would start a business of her own. This, in turn, upset the husband, and he used every behavior he knew to keep her from starting her new adventure. After all, it was his job to keep peace in the family.

But Ruth had done some very hard work inside. She had broken her lifelong commandment about being an obedient wife. This commandment had functioned adequately enough to give her guidance in her early years. She had been a good mother and wife. But at the age of fifty, it was no longer functional. If she kept obeying it when it no longer served a purpose, she would die inside. She was a very vibrant person, and she did not want to give up her creative edge.

Initially, the two commandments of husband and wife interlocked, and they got along well for many years. Now Ruth is dancing to a different beat, and there is clashing between the two. They, of course, were not aware of what was going on inside them. They recognized only that their relationship, which was solid for a long time, was now fragmenting. When they came to see me, they were in a state of disequilibrium. What had been solid was now broken. The predictable was now entering an unexplored potential. The old patterns were breaking down, and the husband was feeling a strong sense of abandonment.

When one person in a relationship begins to make changes within the inner belief systems, it usually shows up in several kinds of altered behaviors outside the normal patterns. When those patterns of change become evident to the mate, there is a very strong desire to force the changing person to return to the way things were when they were stable. The more this pressure is put on the changing partner, the more that partner is required to rebel in order to make the internal changes needed.

Ruth's husband used many different behaviors to make sure that she would stay the same, but none worked. In his exasperation, he joined her in therapy, to see if he could "make her go back to the obedient wife she was." I was not about to buy that, and I required that he take a look at the life commandment he was believing, which required her not to change. As I mentioned above, his belief system required that he keep everyone happy. Now, regardless of what he does, he cannot maintain that belief system. He too must alter his inner gyros and work on abandoning a belief that had been important. Letting go of a cherished belief that has served you for many years is a grieving process. It is like losing a close friend.

The giving up that needs to be done is very often confused with what is going on with the other person. If abandonment is felt, it is not just the awareness that the mate is leaving the cherished patterns, but that something much deeper is going on inside. You are changing also. So the griefs often are mixed up, and it is difficult to know whether you are grieving the loss of an external relationship, or giving up something in yourself, or both at the same time.

Since most of the persons I have interacted with in therapy have relatively little awareness of their own deep belief systems, it takes a lot of emotional courage, on their part, to enter the cavern of their minds and explore the inner space. Most of us have an elusive awareness about the two worlds in which we interact—the world around us and the world within us. But my involvement with people has caused me to believe that many are more aware of the external world than that which is in them. For this reason, it is often difficult to get in touch, and see the inner connection between how we interpret the outer world through the decoding mechanism of our belief systems.

When Ruth's husband saw that she wanted to move into her own business, his internal guidance system decoded the event as being against him. His reaction was that of dominance and control. The consequences were to force Ruth to become more assertive, which, in turn, heightened his anxiety. When such loops are created, it usually takes someone outside the relationship to help them break the cycle.

The couple met with me for more than a year, and both made dramatic changes in the inner rules that guided their lives. Ruth used her new assertiveness to develop a large and profitable business. In the meantime, her husband changed his belief that he needed to keep her happy, because he saw that what she was doing was creative and energizing. In fact, she could make herself joyful. She didn't need him to do that for her.

There was one key issue during this time of change: The dependencies that had developed as a result of the former belief systems now gave way to a deeper maturation of self-confidence and self-determination. The couple was able to keep the marriage together, and both are stronger for it.

The reader should be aware that the emotional effort and struggle these persons went through was significant. Both experienced strong feelings of guilt, anger, anxiety, doubt, rejection, emotional distance, and momentary states of despair. The unusual character of such struggle is that both won. I have, of course, seen other couples and individuals who did not win, because they were not able to make the kinds of internal changes that were necessary.

It is important to note that the usual way we try to make such changes is to force the "other person" to do what we want, rather than go inside ourselves and make the internal correction. If Ruth's husband had been able to keep her from doing what she wanted, he would not have gone through the agony he experienced. But because she stuck to her guns and refused to submit, he was forced to do the hard work, which he needed to do anyway.

I have spun out this rather lengthy example in order to show how complicated the life commandment structure is, and its long-term implications.

The commandments received by inference are difficult to restructure because they are self-imposed. Much of what we believe about ourselves, others, and the world is due to our own conjecture.

One of the positive attributes of such belief systems is that they make us unique. No one else believes what you believe. There certainly are common elements which you have along with me. But I do not possess the same distinctive belief structures as you, because I have not made the same inferences about life's events. Even if we had been at the same place at the same time, what I would infer from that common event and what you would infer most likely would be different. To assume that I must draw, or do draw, the same conclusions you do, would be to add another belief component. That presumes that I have the same kind of information, and the same background as you. Obviously, that is not possible. Consequently, I believe differently from the way you do.

THE HARD WORLD OF ADULTHOOD

Dr. Fritz Kunkle, one of the earliest psychiatrists, believed that we, as adults, carry on our backs a shell like that of a turtle. That shell is made up of *lies that we still believe are truths*, and the function of adult life is to rid ourselves of that shell, so that we come to the end of life knowing only the truth for us.

Ridding ourselves of that shell is hard emotional work and requires intentionality. It will not happen by accident. It means that in order to gain the insight required, we must be able to struggle with that which is within us, explore the inner world of our belief systems and alter them, in order to have an inner belief structure that is appropriate for the tasks that are current in our life. Otherwise, we try to manage the issues of our lives with a belief conceptualization that is inadequate for the current and future tasks and decisions that need to be made.

LIFE COMMANDMENTS BASED ON BEHAVIORS   This type of commandment is content-free. There is no verbalization, only behavior from the commandment giver. Actually, the giver is totally unaware of what is being received by the person interpreting the behavior. In one sense, this commandment form is like that of the inferential commandment, because the observer of the behavior is drawing conclusions that are wholly within the mind of the believer. Let me explain.

When I was a young teenager, and I would begin to show some form of anger or displeasure toward my mother, she would develop a particular look on her face which I interpreted to mean, "How could you be angry at your mother, who took such good care of you." The result of that conclusion was that I believed I should never show anger toward my mother. It was this self-given command that led me to suppress my anger, not only toward my mother, but to most other persons as well.

This leads to a very important understanding. The life commandments which at one time were specific—"Don't get angry at your mother"—are often generalized to the rest of the world. This process, called a generalization, is operative in our lives all the time. If it were not, we would have to learn everything over every day.

For example: Most doorknobs are placed at the opposite side of the door from the hinges. In most cases, this truth works for us consistently and effectively, because most doors operate that way. It is part of our belief system, and we trust it. In experiments on creativity, a group of people were tested to see what they would do when the knob was placed on the same side of the door as the hinge. Each person came and tried the doorknob and found that the door would not open. They pushed and pulled, but the door would not give. Very few tried any other way to open the door. The problem was really simple. All they had to do was push the *other* side of the door, and it would have swung open, since the hinge was like that of a two-way swinging door.

Generalizations are useful, but when they are confronted with situations which require different answers, then the belief system becomes dysfunctional and often does not allow us to look for alternatives, because we believe there are none, other than what we believe. **The only limits we have on what we can do is what we believe we can do**.

Think for a few moments about what you believe, as a result of what you have seen other people do. It is not what they have said, but what they have *done*, and particularly the expressions on their faces. Your interpretation may or may not have been correct. Actually, whether it was correct is not really the issue. The issue is the effect it has had on you and those around you.

Let me try to put some of these elements together to illustrate their power and how they help to form who and what we are and what we can do.

A mother was raising two sons. Part of her belief system was to keep her children from showing arrogance, because people do not like show-offs, she told them.

Her younger son had a special sparkle that drew people to him. As a baby, people would stop and talk to him because he responded with a great deal of energy and gregarious behavior. One day when he was nine, he was dressing in formal clothes for a school concert. With flair of body and impishness in his voice, he said to his mother, "A star is born." His mother responded by slapping him, adding, "Don't be a show-off." He was breaking one of her own life commandments: "People don't like show-offs."

In one moment of time, a life commandment occurred. Though this young man is now an adult, his sparkle is dimmed—not gone altogether, but reduced to a somberness. His mother now knows of life commandments and is aware of what she had done. She now encourages him to use his energy toward more enthusiasm and outgoing behaviors.

Two things can happen when you are more in touch with your own life commandments, and with those you have given to others. First, you can modify them within yourself, so that you do not act on the belief system that would allow you to continue the behavior. And second, you can counter command those you have given to others, in order to give them permission to modify them. You need to know that just hearing the opposite command does not mean that people will believe you and incorporate the new command as quickly as they did the old one.

At the end of this chapter, I will share some of the things you can do to break your own commandments and to help others who are struggling with theirs.

HOW LIFE COMMANDMENTS FORM OUR THEOLOGY

I have had the privilege of training many hundreds of clergy and laity in many denominations. I have done in-depth interviews with these people over a twenty-year period and have found some very helpful things regarding why and what Christians really believe. Because of the in-depth listening skills described in this book, it is possible to go beyond the outward manifestation of Christian faith, to try to understand why they believe what they believe about God and Jesus Christ.

To add to my information, I also have had an opportunity for long-term therapy with pastors and many laypeople. It is the therapy with pastors that has given me the greatest insights into my understanding of how an individual's life commandments shape and determine a person's theology.

Almost without exception, when a pastor is in psychological or theological trouble, a dysfunctional life commandment—a truth that has become a lie—is at the bottom of that difficulty. In this section, I want to explore the effect of our life commandments upon our theological belief system, and what happens to our theological structures when a life commandment is altered, changed, or abandoned.

I reflect again upon two stories referred to at the beginning of this chapter. One woman, abandoned by her mother, was in a large number of foster homes. Since in the beginning of her life she believed that you could not trust the world because it would desert you, that basic belief system affected her theology dramatically. She was basically frightened of God. Understanding God as a loving father was an impossibility for her, because she never had a father. Her experience with men early in her teenage years convinced her that they took from her what they needed and left her stranded. She believed that God would use her, and then drop her from life.

The second illustration is from the woman whose father sent her to the basement if she did not behave at mealtime. When her brother scared her and told her that the devil lived in the basement, she believed that she would some day be sent to hell. She became a fastidious Christian. Everything had to be done just right: You must say all the right prayers, in the right way, at the right time. To not be perfect was cause for her punitive God to send her to perdition. Her life commandment from early childhood was still a part of her adult belief system, and it fashioned her theology. In order to change her distorted belief in God, it was important to change a dysfunctional life commandment. Crazy life commandments produce crazy theology.

One day, a church executive came for therapy. He was seriously questioning his role in the church, and his faith was in serious transition. After several months of therapy, he was able to explore the deeper ramifications of his problem.

He was a workaholic. Spending ten to twelve hours a day, with rarely a day off, he felt driven to be a good Christian and to be liked by everyone. He was experiencing extensive fits of depression and could not seem to shake them. He felt very much driven and stuck. His belief in God was shattering as he said, "I preach each Sunday in a different church, and I am not sure that I believe anything I say anymore."

In examining his belief structures, we finally came to an experience he had when he was a small boy of five. He stated that his bedroom was next to that of his parents, and the walls were thin.

One evening while his parents were fighting in their bedroom, he heard his mother say to his father, "I wish I had never had him. Why did we ever have a child?" It was at that moment that he gave himself his own life commandment (a commandment by inference): "I will always be a good boy. I will make my parents proud of me, even if I'm not wanted." When he told me this, he cried.

The theological extensions of these self-imposed beliefs were dramatized in this pastor's life. He generalized the belief to God. He therefore had to prove to God that he was worthy of God's love. His understanding of divine grace was nil. When pastors under his jurisdiction did not perform as he expected, he became angry. "How is it possible to bring in the kingdom if you don't work at it?"

He had to work to demonstrate to God that he was worthy, for fear he would not be loved. God would love him only to the extent that he performed well. He had little compassion for others if they did not work hard. He drove his pastors, and many of them rebelled at his behavior. Yet he thought of himself as doing what was necessary.

But now things were different. Whatever he did, regardless of how hard he worked, he could not find peace. His inner belief system, at thirty-eight, was no longer functioning. In fact, the more he tried to obey it the worse things became.

Once he was able to get in touch with this belief structure, we were able to talk about other laws that could guide his life, in order to give up the one he could no longer use. After many hours of internal struggle, he came up with a solution. He could "work" at getting a new belief about "grace." But those of us who know about grace know that you cannot *work* at getting it. Grace is not a work, but a gift, and often unexpected. His problem now was learning how to not work and how to be open and pleasant with others, rather than so demanding and rigid.

After a period of six months, he was able to grieve over his dysfunctional belief, a belief on which he had built his life. The very act of letting it go and living with the unknown for a while became very powerful for him. He discovered that he could get close to others without feeling so threatened. He also became aware that he did not need to make everyone happy in order to be OK himself. The belief that you have to please everyone with your behavior is a commandment no one can keep without enormous sacrifice to his or her own well-being.

These beliefs are usually secured before we have developed any concept of God. This will be particularly true of the kinesthetic belief system, secured within the first year of life. It is these internal convictions that help to shape the way we see and understand God.

SCRIPTURES   Once we have developed these deep internal belief systems, we bring them to the Scriptures, where we often proof-text our life commandments. Let me give you a personal example.

I spent twenty-six years as a pastor in the local church. I therefore preached hundreds of sermons. If you had heard me preach at that time, you would have been aware of a rather consistent theme in my preaching. It would sound like this:

> My friends in Christ. As we gather this morning to worship our Lord, it may be that we will not be able to come to the joy that we all may want. But that is not what is important. What we need to do is to be faithful to Christ, regardless of what happens to us. There is no guarantee that we ever will be happy.

In that statement, you should be able to hear the life commandment I received from my mother: "You can never expect to be happy in this life." And I preached that for many years.

The gospel I was preaching was the gospel according to Edna (my mother). Do you know what we call it when we are following the wrong god? Idolatry! I had been believing the wrong God!

After breaking that commandment from my mother, I now have a different theology, based on a new text: "That you may have life, and have it more abundantly." During all those years, I had never preached on that text. Why? It was against my earlier life commandment. If you are a pastor, you may want to look at texts upon which you have never preached, to see if there is a common theme. It may give you a clue to your internal commandments.

RELIGIOUS LANGUAGE   Language is a representational system which gives distinctive clues from the unconscious. By listening to religious language, you also can find specific indicators of what people are struggling with deep within themselves.

In a very unique research project several years ago, Dr. Edgar Draper of Chicago, and four other psychiatrists, set out to prove that one could tell people's psychological difficulty by listening to their theology. They opened the file drawers from their clinic and randomly picked fifty persons to be interviewed. Two of the doctors asked these fifty persons thirteen religious questions, such as:

"What is your favorite book in the Bible, and why?"

"Who is your favorite character in the Bible, and why?"

"If God would grant you three requests, what would they be?"

"Do you pray? What do you usually pray about?"

The two interviewing doctors, who did not know the patients, wrote verbatims on the answers the clients gave. Two other doctors read the answers and deduced what they believed to be the diagnostic evaluation in the clinical charts. A fifth doctor checked their evaluations against the diagnosis in the charts, and found that they were right in 96.8 percent of the cases.

Dr. Edgar Draper, a former pastor, thought that the psychiatric world should be told to ask their patients to talk about their beliefs, because it could lead to deeper insights into their lives.

It is easier to note psychological distortions by listening to theological maladjustment. When religious experience is used to protect and distort the person's reality, it is possible to get to the life commandments more quickly, and with less resistance.

A local internist called me to refer a patient, because he could not tolerate the person's religious language. He virtually did not know how to respond to it appropriately, or how to use it to help her. Most medical schools do not deal with religious phenomenology. I agreed to see the woman, who was in her late forties, and she came to see me several days later. After she was seated in my office, the following dialogue took place:

"What caused you to come to see me?"

"Jesus told me to come see you."

"I'm glad Jesus told you to come and see me. Why do you think Jesus told you to come?"

She did not answer my question, but said, "I love my Jesus, you know."

"It's good to love Jesus. In what ways do you love Jesus?"

"Well, when I get up in the morning, I ask Jesus what I should put on, and Jesus always tells me. When I go down to get breakfast for my family—you know I have a husband and an eleven-year-old son who still wets his bed; when he does that, I make him kneel down by his bed and confess his sins to Jesus—I always ask Jesus what I should have for breakfast, and he always tells me. You know I really love my Jesus."

By now, you might suspect that there is something not quite right about this woman's theology and belief system. Her overuse of the word *Jesus*, her inability to make decisions on her own, but relying completely on Jesus, should send signals that behind that language, there is a life commandment which acts as an internal drive.

Two and a half years before this woman came to see me, she had been suffering from deep depression. One late evening, after her thirteenth attempt to commit suicide, she said that Jesus had stood at the end of her bed, "lit up like a neon light." The experience so frightened her that she stopped having suicidal thoughts and went around from church to church, telling others how Jesus had healed her. However, as a result of a bad verbal fight with her husband, she had begun to have fleeting thoughts of suicide again. These thoughts frightened her, and she again sought help for her problem.

After many sessions, we finally got to the deep inner belief system. During one session, I asked, "Who are you, deep inside there, anyway? I have worked with you for many months, and I don't know who you are. Who are you, deep behind your religious language?"

She flushed, became angry, and began to cry. In the midst of her tears, she said softly, "I am a nobody, I am a nobody."

When listening to religious language, be sure to be aware of single words that are repeated again and again. These become the themes not only of the person's meta-story, but also are the doorways to life commandments, although the storyteller usually is not conscious of this language.

This awareness allowed us to move into a life commandment that was difficult both for her to tell and for me to hear. In her family, girls had been treated as nonentities. She was told many times that she was worth nothing, that she was not lovable and would amount to nothing. One day the inevitable occurred, and she believed it.

Many years later, as a result of going to church on a regular basis, she found that her priest was a person she could trust, and because he loved Jesus, she found that she could, too. As a result of that religious experience, she developed an overwhelming dependency upon Jesus and was not able to let go. Much of her theology was a reaction to her deeper belief system, which at her age was now dysfunctional.

Now comes the sad part. After this woman discovered what she believed about herself, she was unwilling to change. She believed that if she changed what she believed, Jesus would leave her, and she could not give up her love for her Lord.

Something new emerged as a result of this conversation. The way she had received response from her parents was to believe that she was nothing. If she had thought more highly of herself, she believed that her parents would not love her. Since Jesus often is a parent figure for some people, the generalization is made, and the truth of the first premise is transferred to all similar situations.

The most difficult part of this scenario is that a religious experience helps to perpetuate the dysfunctional life commandment. Because if you change the deeper structure of your belief system, you will have to alter your religious understanding of the nature of God, or, in the case of this woman, the way she relates to Jesus. The end result of this particular counseling was that the woman felt that I was trying to make her give up her faith in Jesus, and she stopped coming.

The interactive relationship between the inner belief structure and the religious understanding bind each other, and thus cause the dysfunction to continue. The really hard religious work is the ability to let go of your theological comprehension, in order to find a new one. This takes a deeper understanding of faith—that is, the ability to believe in God while you are not believing in God. Or, as Paul put it, "I believe; help my unbelief!" (Mark 9:24).

In reshaping people's lives to give them new life, there must be a different inner law. As Jesus succinctly put it, "I give you a new commandment" (John 13:34). "I came that they may have life, and have it abundantly" (John 10:10b).

SUMMARY

A Strategy for Changing a Dysfunctional Belief in Yourself or Another:

Kinesthetic Belief: I believe what I feel.

Verbal Commands: I believe what others tell me about myself and the world.

Inferences: I believe that what I say to myself equals the truth.

Behaviors: I believe that what I see others model for me is what I can, must, or want to become.

Generalizations: I believe that when one thing is true, then other things like it also must be true.

Theological Implications: What I believe about myself and the world influences what I believe about God.

Neuro-Linguistic Programming (NLP) is a relatively new method of psychotherapy. Because NLP has developed into a very large area of study, I deal here only with some of the parts that will help a person listen and communicate. Translated, its name literally means "language of the nervous system." The method was developed by Richard Bandler, John Grinder, Leslie Cameron Bandler, Judith Delozier, Robert Dilts, David Gordon, and others. It includes and is rich with behavioral technology made applicable to the psychotherapist, as well as being useful to any encounter that involves communication—education, managment, sales, and so on.

NLP is the study of the structure of subjective experience . . . and intersects with the theoretical material of several fields, including Cybernetics, Linguistics, Psychotherapy, and personality theory. NLP makes explicit patterns of behavior and change that have previously been only intuitively understandable.

THE LINGUISTIC BRIDGE

Neuro-Linguistic Programming

NLP is the study of subjective experiences.

Bandler and Grinder based much of their work on the theories of Gregory Bateson. They also studied successful therapists such as Virginia Satir, Fritz Perls, and Rollo May, to discover the patterns of their success. They drew from a variety of therapies already established, developed their own jargon, and these initial studies resulted in NLP.

THEORY/MODEL

Neuro-Linguistic Programming uses models more than theory as a means to guide clients through processes to help them reach desired states.

A theory is a tentative statement that attempts to explain or interpret WHY things relate as they do. A model, however, is a pattern or copy of already existing phenomena which, as designed, can be imitated or recreated. . . . Any model of human experience is designed to be specific and empirical. It is based on what we can see, hear, feel, smell, etc.

In Neuro-Linguistic Programming theory, the nature of people is neutral. A healthy person makes use of internal and external resources to reach goals and solve problems. Illness is not being aware of or not using available resources. People can change by using internal and external resources to solve their problems, and the therapist helps them do this by using specific strategies designed to use those resources.

USING REPRESENTATIONAL SYSTEMS TO BUILD RAPPORT

Representational systems are the internal and external pictures, sounds, words, and feelings that we use to represent and make sense of the world. In other words, we interpret and experience the world through our senses. Most of us have a primary, or lead, representational system, our most highly valued and most conscious sensory channel at any point in time. We tend to favor that system especially during times of stress.

LANGUAGE   We also unconsciously choose language to represent the system we favor at the moment. For example, the "visual" person might say, "I *see* what you mean," or "That's *clear* to me."

On the other hand, an "auditory" person might say, "That really *clicked* for me," or "It *sounds* good to me!"

The "kinesthetic" or "feeling" person is usually in touch with emotions and can name them, such as, "I *feel* very *anxious* about what is happening here," or "I was *touched* by that experience."

Olfactory (taste and smell) might sound like, "This experience has left a *bad taste* in my mouth," or "I *smell* something rotten going on."

Some predicates (verbs, adverbs, and adjectives) can be used to indicate the visual representational system: *bright, clear, colorful, focus, glimpse, hazy, peek, perspective, picture, pretty,* and *show.*

A sampling of auditory predicates might be *call, discuss, harmony, hear, listen, loud, noisy, shout, talk, tell,* and *yell.*

Kinesthetic predicates could be represented by the words *clumsy, concrete, feel, firm, hurt, irritated, pressure, pushy, relaxed, tense, touch,* and *touchy.*

What does this have to do with the listener? How can we find this useful?

The listener can build rapport quickly by matching the representational system of the speaker. One can literally be speaking the speaker's language. Matching the language also removes barriers to understanding. It helps the listener to be more aware of how the person organizes and interprets his or her world.

To illustrate how this might be used in a listening setting, suppose that a friend comes in and describes her problem this way: "My daughter has just told me that she is pregnant and plans to drop out of school. I am so hurt that she would let this happen. I have tried to be firm but loving. I guess I've failed as a parent, or this would not have happened."

The listener replies, "Let me see if I'm clear on this. You picture yourself as a failure because of your daughter's situation. Is that your perspective?

The client replies, "Well, I'm not sure, but I know I just feel terrible."

The therapist and client are using two different language structures; they are speaking different languages. This creates a barrier to building rapport and understanding.

If the therapist were to respond with kinesthetic rather than visual predicates, the relationship could be established much more quickly: "My guess is that you are experiencing a great deal of pain and confusion over this situation, right?"

The client probably would reply, "Exactly." Now they can move on instead of getting hung up at an impasse.

MIRRORING   Another method of rapport building used in NLP is "mirroring." Mirroring is "matching a person's posture, gestures, rate of breathing, etc." (Lewis and Pucelik, 1982). Some people do this quite intuitively. It is reported that Virginia Satir mirrored naturally. If a person with a certain accent came in, she would match the accent slightly. Mirroring puts the client at ease because the unconscious recognizes that "this person is like me," but the conscious usually does not notice the actual behavior.

There are several ways rapport can be built with the mirroring behaviors. Matching the tone of the other, breathing at the same rate, picking up on the rhythm and matching it with a part of your body movement— that is, nodding your head, moving a finger, moving the foot, speaking in the same rhythm, and matching the body posture.

The purpose of these behaviors is to reduce the possibility that the speaker will perceive you as uninterested or not caring. I usually build rapport quite easily, but on occasion I do not, and I usually pay a high price for the broken rapport.

I had completed a short workshop for a group of hospice volunteers, when a member of the group asked me if I had ever trained insurance agents in how to listen to their clients. I said that I had, and he later called and invited me to meet for lunch with his boss, the president of a large insurance agency, another agent, and himself. As I was introduced to the president of the agency, he told me that he was also looking for a person to speak at a national insurance convention. I said to myself, "This could be an important meeting; maybe I can get that job."

The president sat next to me on a bench that faced out into the room. The other two men were across the table. As the conversation began, I was aware that the president was sitting so that his body was square to me. He did not turn his head or his body when he talked to me, but looked straight ahead. His language was auditory, and he used no visual or kinesthetic representational language. His tone was harsh, his language clipped in short, brief statements. My inference from his behavior was that he did not want to be there.

Since I rarely use those types of behaviors, I found myself mismatching him. Then I did a very inappropriate thing in trying to bridge to this man's world. I turned toward him, leaned slightly forward, and used a warm tone of voice. But he only became more rigid, with a more intense tone that verged on hostile, and I began to feel a bit intimidated. He became critical of what I was saying and began to push me to tell him exactly why he should hire me to train his people. I struggled to answer his questions, but he was not satisfied with my comments.

It became obvious after the luncheon was over that I had broken rapport with him several times. The problem was that I had done what I teach others not to do—that if something does not work, don't keep doing it! Change. The more I had turned to him, mismatching behaviors, the more hostile he had become.

I did not get the job. I remember feeling that I had missed a very good opportunity to break into training people in the insurance business.

I share this experience to let you know the price you may pay if you do not build correct rapport. I learned a great deal from that encounter. In fact, I will never forget it. It was a great teaching moment for me, and it has not happened again. I know now to match, though mildly, the behaviors of others, in order to bridge to their world. The most crucial thing that NLP teaches is that to communicate with other human beings, you must enter their world through **their** communication system.

TESTING RAPPORT   How do you know when rapport has been built? You can make a very simple test. Make some simple move, and see if the speaker does what you do. When listening to another, I often make a deliberate move to see if the other will follow. I might scratch my knee or rub my cheek or nose. Usually within a minute, the speaker will use the same behavior, though not necessarily at the same place. I might scratch my knee, but the person might scratch the head or arm. Once I have tested that rapport has been built, I can then concentrate on other issues of the relationship.

USING NLP PREDICATES TO REDUCE CONFLICT

Conflict management skills are more effective when combined with NLP. I am very aware that when people mismatch their language structures, they often feel that the other person is uncooperative and emotionally distant.

Imagine that three people are meeting to work out the direction and purposes of their organization. One of them is auditory dominate, another visual, and the third kinesthetic. The conversation might go something like this:

> **Auditory**: I was *told* that I was to lead this meeting, so I want to *hear* what the two of you have to *say*. It sort of *clicked* for me, as I was *listening* to the radio this morning, what we might do to get this church off the plateau. But I want to *hear* your ideas first, so *talk* to me about what you think.
>
> **Visual**: I guess I don't *see* that as being the issue. From my *perspective*, we have lost *sight* of our original goals. Everything is kind of *fuzzy* for me. In fact, I have been having a dim *view* of this place lately. I can *picture* this place going down the tubes, if we can't get our *vision* more clearly developed. I can *see* us putting a big poster out in the hallway, *showing* the people the direction we need to go. What do you *see* us doing?

Kinesthetic: I don't know what the two of you are *experiencing* here, but *I feel discouraged* most of the time. We used to be such a *close* working group. I am having difficulty getting a *handle* on what has gone wrong. We don't seem to be able to work out our problems because we're *out of touch* with one another. Yesterday, after a meeting I attended where everything *fell apart*, I went home with a bad *taste* in my mouth. I'm actually *confused* about what we should do.

It should be obvious that if these persons stay in their own communication modes, without bridging to the others' worlds, conflict in the form of misunderstanding would rapidly occur.

Each of us tends to have a preferred dominance in the language structure we use. This occurs because during our childhood and teenage years, we were given commands (like life commandments) that gave our brains permission to use those channels to recall and filter our experiences.

If you were scolded every time you came up with an idea and told that you were dumb, or didn't know what you were talking about, you would stop talking about what you were thinking, and would often go silent. You might say to yourself what you wanted to say, but you would not say it to someone else.

I personally learned how to shut off the verbal channel in my early childhood; it was a way of avoiding the critical sound of my father's voice. To this day I often do not say what I am thinking or feeling, even when it would be appropriate to do so. However, I am much better at saying what I am thinking than in previous years.

Other persons will not be able to see what is going on in their world because they were not permitted to become observers of their internal or external world. Those with closed visual channels have lost the discrimination of visual access clues. They then miss nonverbal behaviors and often act inappropriately.

Some time ago, my wife and I met with a salesman in our home who was trying to sell us a service that would stop moisture from coming through the walls of our basement. He did a very thorough inspection and his verbal presentation was excellent. He drew charts and diagrams that were clear and precise. All of this took about two hours—much longer than we had anticipated.

After his presentation, we asked about the cost. The expenses were going to be more than we had anticipated, so we told him we needed some time to think about it. I stood up and said that I needed to go to another appointment. My wife stood up, but he continued to try to sell us the job. I then told him I felt that I was being pushed. He still did not stop his sales pitch. Finally, I told him we would call him later. He then stood up, still trying to sell us the job. We walked to the door, I opened it, and he left. He did not get the job.

This is a typical case of the loss of visual acuity. Had he been aware of our nonverbal behavior, that we were anxious about the price and had stood up, he would not have pushed us to the point of resistance. It is a common sales error at the closing of the sale.

Another type of language from the kinesthetic channel is frequently shut down in our culture—reluctance to experience our own feelings and be in touch with our own internal world. From my experience as a listener, I am aware that men are less likely than women to be in touch with their own feelings. These commands given to little boys—"Big boys don't cry," "Don't be a sissy," "Be macho"—which can be interpreted as "Don't feel." When the kinesthetic channel is shut down, we lose an important part of the feedback system about our own life. Because most of our feelings come from the right brain, intuition is blocked, so that our ability to know without knowing is missing.

This can be recognized when you are listening to another and you note that most of, if not all the kinesthetic language is missing. The effective listener listens not only to what is said, but for what is missing.

The missing language tells you the location of the person's personal pain, for it usually is in the closed channel(s). That is why it is difficult for some people to talk about their pain. They do not have the language to describe it.

If you find that the language of a given channel is completely missing, it is most likely that the channel was shut down before the development of language. If this has occurred, it will be more difficult to use the missing language, because it will be less comprehensible to the speaker.

IMPLICATIONS FOR EDUCATION

I have trained teachers and principals of school systems in these listening skills, including NLP. Each teacher has found the implications very helpful in teaching a child, teenager, or adult through the channels that are most developed and helping them open the channels they have shut down.

Imagine what happens when an auditory-dominant teacher tries to communicate with a group of visual/kinesthetic-dominant children. The children want to see what the teacher is talking about, or at least to experience in some way what the teacher is saying, not just listen to a lecture.

A FAMILY'S MISMATCHED BEHAVIOR   I had a most interesting experience with a family during one of my training events. This may illustrate the problem of trying to communicate when the channels do not match.

I rarely stay in the home of a client when I am out on the road. But I made an exception in this particular case, because they had a private mother-in-law apartment attached to their home, and I agreed to stay there. I did, however, eat breakfast with the family.

On the second day of the five-day training event, when I entered the kitchen, the wife asked if I would be willing to talk to their sixteen-year-old daughter. She was flunking out of science, and they did not know how to get her to do her assignments. She had an oral exam the next day and was not ready for it. I had met the teenager and was impressed with her ability to communicate with me, but was aware that she did not communicate well with her parents.

I agreed to meet with the teenager, but also asked that the parents be present. I wanted to see if they were doing something that contributed to their daughter's problem.

That evening we sat in their living room to talk about the problem. This is how the conversation started:

JOHN: What seems to be the problem?
FATHER: I have been *telling* this girl for the last six weeks to get ready for this assignment, but she will not *listen* to me. I have *told* her over and over again, but she just keeps putting it off.
MOTHER: I have been *telling* her the same thing, and she doesn't *listen* to me, either.

Both parents were auditory dominant!

As the parents spoke, the daughter looked up toward her left and folded her arms across her chest. (Eye movements up toward the speaker's right indicate visual internal accessing.)

I asked the daughter if she would **show** me tomorrow's assignment.

She agreed, left the room, and in a moment returned with her book, a beautiful, full color, glossy manual. She showed me the pages of the assignment. She was taking a course in anatomy and had to tell the class how the blood flows from one organ to another. I asked her if she understood what the pictures meant. She was able to show me step by step, by pointing to the picture, how the blood flowed. She did know the subject.

I knew that her dad had a color copier at his office, so I asked her if she could imagine blowing up the pictures on his copier and hanging them on a set of coat hangers, making a mobile out of it. I told her that all she had to do was to hang the mobile in front of the class and *show* the class how the blood flows.

Her eyes opened wider, and she said, "Oh, I can do that!" She turned to her father and asked for the car keys.

Her father asked me why she would attempt the project for me and not for him. After the daughter left, I explained something of the language problem that I heard during his communication with his daughter.

The following day, the teenager came in grinning like a Cheshire cat, saying she had gotten an "A." The teacher had told her it was one of the most creative reports in the class.

Human communication requires that we match the other person's linguistic strategies. It is simply the act of matching other people's worlds, so that we can make a bridge to their reality.

SUMMARY

The NLP bridge is the ability to match the speaker's linguistic structure. This is done by using the same kinesthetic, auditory, or visual language as that used by the speaker.

Index